Praise for Griffith Review

'*Griffith Review* continues as the lodestar for what we can expect in excellent Australian writing.'

Melissa Lucashenko, author

'In just over two decades, *Griffith Review* has mounted guard over Australian letters in a way that no other publication – established or new – has been able to replicate. In a world where critics and commentators too often talk across each other, its focused, topic-based approach has cleared a space for genuine engagement, recalling us to the (retreating) ideal of a living intellectual culture.' Richard King, writer and critic

'*Griffith Review* is the sound of Australian democracy and culture thinking out loud.' Geordie Williamson, *The Australian*

'*Griffith Review* is my quarterly literary feast. I have discovered many new favourite writers and ideas between its covers.'

Sharlene Allsopp, author

'[*Griffith Review*] traverses genre and form, culture and continent… in what is a vibrant and impressive cross-section of modern Australian writing.' *Good Reading*

'…informative, thought-provoking and well-crafted.'

The Saturday Paper

'It turned out that the only place we could write the truth that was in our hearts was in literary journals like *Griffith Review*, that everywhere else, we were stifled into silence – but here a poem, an essay, a story that said what was painful to admit.' Yumna Kassab, author

'This quarterly magazine is a reminder of the breadth and talent of Australian writers. Verdict: literary treat.' *Herald Sun*

'This is commentary of a high order. The prose is unfailingly polished; the knowledge and expertise of the writers impressive.'

Roy Williams, *Sydney Morning Herald*

SIR SAMUEL GRIFFITH was one of Australia's notable early achievers. He occupied positions of authority during some of the most momentous events in the history of Queensland: the frontier wars, the 'blackbirding' trade of people from Melanesia, the shearers' strike and Federation. At times he challenged power, at others he used it – he was a complex yet pragmatic man of words, a man of his times. Not all his decisions have stood the test of time. Sir Samuel was twice the premier of Queensland, its chief justice and author of its criminal code, remembered most for his pivotal role in drafting the Constitution adopted at Federation, and as the new nation's first chief justice.

Griffith died in 1920 and is now most likely to be remembered by his namesakes: an electorate, a society, a suburb and a university. In 1971, ninety-six years after he first proposed establishing a university in Brisbane, Griffith University, the city's second, was created. Griffith's commitment to public debate and ideas, his delight in words and art, and his attachment to active citizenship are recognised by this publication that bears his name.

Like Sir Samuel Griffith, *Griffith Review* is iconoclastic and non-partisan, with a sceptical eye and a pragmatically reforming heart. Always ready to debate ideas. Personal, political and unpredictable, it informs and provokes Australia's best conversations.

During Griffith's lifetime, and while he was in positions of power, the First Nations of Queensland resisted invasion. Sir Samuel made it possible for some Aboriginal people to testify in court when charges were brought against settlers. The First Australians survived, but at a terrible cost. In the twenty-first century, the need for a thorough and lasting settlement is urgent, one that respects and honours the rights, history and culture of the descendants of those who were dispossessed.

Griffith Review staff acknowledge and pay particular respect to the traditional custodians of the lands on which their office is located, the Jagera and Turrbal people in South-East Queensland.

GriffithReview91

On the Money

Edited by Carody Culver
Contributing Editor: Daniel Nour

GriffithReview91

INTRODUCTION

NON-FICTION

IN CONVERSATION

Peter Bakacs, *2x2* (2023),
acrylic on canvas, 1,125 x 912 mm
Courtesy of the artist

Griffith Review gratefully acknowledges the support and generosity of our founding patron, the late Margaret Mittelheuser AM and the ongoing support of Dr Cathryn Mittelheuser AM.

GriffithReview91 2026
Griffith Review is published four times a year by Griffith University.

Publisher	Scott Harrison
Editor	Carody Culver
General Manager	Katie Woods
Deputy Editor	Amber Gwynne
Editorial Assistant	Darby Jones
Typesetting	Midland Typesetters
Printing	Ligare Book Printers
Distribution	NewSouth Books/ADS

ISBNs
Book: 978-1-923213-16-6
PDF: 978-1-923213-17-3
Epub: 978-1-923213-18-0

ISSN 1448-2924

GRIFFITH REVIEW
South Bank Campus, Griffith University
PO Box 3370, South Brisbane QLD 4101 Australia
Ph +617 3735 3071 Fax +617 3735 3272
griffithreview@griffith.edu.au griffithreview.com

SUBSCRIPTIONS: See griffithreview.com

FEEDBACK AND COMMENT griffithreview@griffith.edu.au

INTRODUCTION

Undisclosed funds

What we talk about when we (can't) talk about money

Carody Culver

IN 2022, THE American culture writer Jordan Calhoun penned a column in *The Atlantic* that I still think about. In his piece, Calhoun recalls the financial precarity of his college years, where he began 'the first of many adventures being surrounded by people I felt were rich while I pretended not to be poor': stealing food when his study allowance ran out, scanning the pages of textbooks in a bookshop when he couldn't afford to buy his own copies. No one he knew talked openly about their income or spending habits – so as Calhoun grew older and sought to overcome his ongoing struggles with money, he turned to pop culture in the hope of gaining insight into what '"normal" finances' looked like.

No deal: film and TV characters, he realised, tend to talk around money or blur its contours; this fiscal coyness is so entrenched that it's become a trope: *undisclosed funds*. In *Friends*, recovering rich girl Rachel gasps in dismay at her first Central Perk paycheque, but we never glean the amount; in *Succession*, the Roy family, who exists in a wealth-cushioned cocoon of moral turpitude, speaks in economic abstractions or discusses figures so inconceivably huge that they're rendered meaningless to the average viewer.

The reason Calhoun's piece has lodged itself so stubbornly in my mind is that I, like him, entered early adulthood with no sense of how other people *did* money and a burning desire to find out. This desire has been largely cultivated by my own catastrophic financial instincts alongside the confounding sense that everyone I know has an innate ability to live within their means while I'm usually sweating bullets until next payday. Like Calhoun, I'm also desperate for cold, hard numbers rather than subtler codes of prosperity or penury. Yet all I've really learnt from the hours I've spent scrolling through posts about earnings and expenditure in Reddit's r/AusFinance community is that whatever your income is, and however you choose to (or have to) spend it, someone, somewhere, is going to judge you.

IN THE SPIRIT of, shall we say, more emotionally open accounting, this edition of *Griffith Review* seeks to lay the books bare. The essays, fiction, conversations, poetry and visual art in *On the Money* expose the complications and contradictions of our relationship with capital and cash. You'll discover the alarming schism between banking and democracy; rethink the way Australia funds literature; explore the connection between teeth and poverty; consider the manifold moral failures of effective altruism; delve into Big Tech's neocolonial machinations; gain new perspectives on volunteering, universal basic income and the economics of care work; chart the complexities of class and status in the publishing and legal professions; be amazed by how tax reform can change the world; learn what meme coins may mean for the future of money; and so much more. *On the Money* also features the first of our remarkable 2025 Emerging Voices competition winners: Miriam Webster's striking and surreal short story, 'The real deal'.

This edition's contributing editor is the wonderful Daniel Nour, an author, journalist and member of Sweatshop Literacy Movement; he commissioned a visceral and affecting short story by emerging writer Victor Guan Yi Zhou. Daniel and Victor, it was a delight to work with you both and to help realise your vision for this piece. Team GR is also very grateful to the Copyright Agency Cultural Fund for its support of our contributing editor project in 2026.

Perhaps one day I'll be good with money; in the meantime, I'm happy to keep reading about it, and I hope you are, too. Whether you picked up this edition via your subscription (thank you!), bought it from a bookshop, borrowed it from a mate, checked it out of the library or found it abandoned at a bus stop, I can guarantee you'll get literary bang for your buck.

– December 2025

NON-FICTION

Let's talk about tax, baby

How economic reform can change the world

Abi Stephenson

IN THE WORLD of tax, double entendres are much like SmashMouth years: they start coming and they don't stop coming. Even tax accountants and treasury economists must groan upon hearing the ding of a *Let's Get Fiscal* webinar invite. When the book *The Joy of Tax: How a fair tax system can create a better society* came out in 2015, *Guardian* journalist Zoe Williams interviewed its author, chartered-accountant-turned-wonk Richard Murphy:

> 'Tax is, anyway, the second most interesting word ending in x in the English language,' he tells me, in case I hadn't got the fact that it sounds a bit like 'sex' from the title of the book. This is what it does to a person, when they spend more than a decade trying to persuade the world that tax is actually a fun thing to talk about.

It may be fifty shades of boring to most of us, but by all rights tax reform should be *the* water-cooler topic *du jour.* Despite the many damning reports about our ongoing cost-of-living crisis, Oxfam found in 2024 that in Australia, billionaires have increased their wealth by 70.5 per cent or $120 billion since 2020. Most Australians are on a very different trajectory. The simple aspiration to independently own a place to live is now beyond the reach of the next generation, with median house prices soaring to at least eight times the average income. As Alan Kohler argues in his new book on the housing crisis, we've already sold off the level playing field that was once the bedrock of the ubiquitous Australian 'fair go'.

Three quarters of Australians support a wealth tax, with similar levels of support in the UK and the US, but amazingly, introducing one remains political suicide – even on the left. In wealthy countries like ours, where democracy is being eroded by tech oligarchs, where media monopolies and basic human rights including housing, food and healthcare are increasingly not assured, voters still reject the idea of ambitious, paradigm-shifting policymaking that might make things better. Why?

In the US, Elizabeth Warren and Bernie Sanders floated super-wealth taxes, and the 'too liberal' presidential candidates sank in rapid succession. In the UK, Thomas Piketty and a handful of other renowned economists recently wrote a public letter to the Labour government proposing a wealth tax, but it's very unlikely this policy will fly there either. When the Australian Greens proposed a 'Robin Hood' tax on billionaires in 2024, it was dismissed as a 'fairytale policy'; even Labor's Jim Chalmers laughed it off as a 'bid for attention'. Lumped in a big pile of undergraduate cringe with Adam Bandt's German house DJ sets and giant toothbrush stunts, the policy's reputation was summarily swept away with the former leader's seat.

If people who are struggling to put food on the table aren't voting for a policy that taxes superyacht owners more, then the problem lies with the sales pitch, not the policy. Tax is arguably the most powerful lever we have to ensure we can still call ourselves an egalitarian meritocracy and keep a straight face. Labor now has an overwhelming post-election mandate and an oft-vaunted vision to deliver a fairer future for all. If this isn't the time for fresh, brave policy ideas, when is?

Despite pressure on tax reform from the Australian Council of Trade Unions' Sally McManus, Chalmers' August 2025 roundtable successes were modest indeed, and the changes won't have troubled many pub chats. As culpable as our leaders are, the calls are coming from inside the house, too. With our cognitive biases and frailties making us loath to investigate the grey tax blob, it's hardly any wonder that, as Nobel Prize–winning economist Jean Tirole has put it, 'each successive government postpones the tax revolution' – and change never comes.

MY FORMER THINK tank colleagues and I used to call this type of policy arena 'a bit PMS' – aka *pale*, *male* and *stale*. A few years before he was embraced by Jeremy Corbyn's economics team, we actually invited the punning 'Joy of Tax' taxpert to speak at an event about social justice and tax reform. A few audience members lost the battle to remain conscious by slide five, and my jaw ached from maintaining a supportive smile from the front row. It *was* world-changing stuff, but you'd rather watch a swatch of 'Elephant's Breath Grey' drying on a wall. No one recognised the revolution when it came because it was wearing rimless glasses and mumbling about a global tax architecture.

If I were a global supervillain intent on shoring up my ill-gotten gains, where would I hide the piece of the puzzle that could cause my downfall? As any keen reader of Greek myth or *Nancy Drew* knows, the best place to conceal something is in plain sight. The word 'tax' is the ultimate anti-clickbait; nothing is less likely to get the Average Joel to the barricades than a three-week conference on 'progressive taxation for an inclusive and just social organisation of care'. Despite sharing very little in common with the astronomically wealthy supergroup, Joel (along with most of us) is on the side of The Beatles and not the dreaded 'taxman' (who was at that time collecting a top tax rate of 90 per cent – absolutely unthinkable to most billionaires today).

It's not just boredom. Many of us are enculturated to feel that taxation is inherently unfair. I still remember the sense of injustice I felt when I opened my first waitressing paycheque and discovered that a sizeable chunk had been subtracted before it hit my wallet. It was many years before I received any kind of tax 'education' at all, and years after that when I first heard the phrase 'people want Scandinavian welfare on American taxes'.

Just the other week, a tradie who fixed my fence complained that he couldn't afford to lose any more to the taxman, and I'm sure he's right. There aren't many who'd willingly give a larger proportion of their personal income away to secure anonymous collective futures. We know from Daniel Kahneman's work on prospect theory that humans are loss-averse: we resent losing a dollar far more than we love winning one. So, when a politician utters the magic term 'tax cuts' during election season, it sounds fabulous to just about everyone – even those to whom tax cuts won't apply. Small business owners who find themselves struggling at tax time mistakenly conflate themselves with big corporations and see all mention of 'good for business' as referring to the same sort of apples.

But most of us don't benefit from tax cuts the way we think. In his 2018 book *Can Democracy Survive Global Capitalism?*, Robert Kuttner describes the international race to the bottom with tax cuts – in the UK under Thatcher in the '80s, the top tax rate on wages went from 83 per cent to 60 per cent, and then down to 40 per cent. It was similar in the US under Reagan. And, of course, in a globalised economy, where one goes the others must follow. Despite being one of the richest countries in the OECD, Australia is one of its lowest taxing countries, and our poverty level is higher than average. Where we once accepted higher marginal tax rates on the highest incomes as standard, today the new normal – more than half as little – has become almost impossible to budge. Even Chalmers' modest proposal to decrease the tax concessions for superannuation funds over $3 million was met with a wave of fury from the press. 'We'll tax you till you're poor' read the headline on 9news.com.au. The 'you' in question is, quite naturally, not the average reader – 99.5 per cent of Australians don't have anything like that amount in their superannuation funds. However, as long as the reader thinks this headline speaks directly to them and their stretched resources, there's no need to read any further. When it's impossible just to reduce a tax break, let alone increase a levy, it's a truly Sisyphean task for any politician.

But the hits keep on coming, because tax is not only boring and unfair-seeming; it's also baffling. In bandying about terms like 'flagship financial security index' and 'illicit financial flows vulnerability tracker', even the laudable Tax Justice Network struggles to engage the average punter in important discourse that affects their daily lives. It's a dispiriting sea of word clouds, bad logos and jargon, even from the reformers themselves.

There's a more sinister side to this bafflement – language can be used to deliberately obscure. Richard Denniss of The Australia Institute describes it as 'econobabble': internal lingo used outside the system to consciously flummox and ward off interaction. If one lobs a 'macroprudential liquidity coverage ratio' or 'countercyclical equity capital buffers' into the chat, one can quickly shut down any would-be meddlers in economic orthodoxies. Economics should be for everyone, as the economist Ha-Joon Chang has spent the lion's share of his career trying to point out. It's just that economists have been very successful at making out it's all far too difficult for the average citizen to understand. They've also persuaded many of us that economics is an empirical science with ungovernable, immutable natural rules rather than a set of theories greatly influenced by different political values and viewpoints.

So, in the absence of widespread confidence in what we're talking about, whoever can build the most persuasive top-line narrative wins the debate. Historically, the right wing has managed to completely dominate the 'good with money' space. Just like the kids' mnemonic for unscrewing something, the economic idea of 'lefty loosey, righty tighty' is deeply embedded in our consciousness. The left is chaotic and idealistic: a bunch of dreadlocked bleeding hearts who will kill business and tank the economy. The right is a safe pair of grown-up hands: this lot wears suits, supports the conditions for the creation of wealth, and will bring more money that will eventually, ahem, *trickle down*. (Even Pope Francis regularly condemned trickle-down economics, calling the idea a 'crude and naive trust in the goodness of those wielding economic power' and counselling against an economy of inequality and exclusion, for 'such an economy kills'.)

But misinformation is rife, as the bulk of Australians bounce between Murdoch-dominated news sources (Siri, please show me a media giant who might have a vested interest in tax cuts?) and social media, where more Australians now get their news than from traditional media. We're being regularly manipulated with false narratives about where our hard-earned tax dollars end up – in the pockets of 'dole bludgers' and not-seeking jobseekers stuck in a poverty trap. Such cynical witch hunts contributed to the robodebt scandal, the supposed crackdown, on taypayers' behalf, on welfare rorters that spawned suicides and required a royal commission and millions of dollars of compensation. Yet a huge proportion of the welfare bill actually goes towards pensions and services for older Australians, and the rest towards industries and infrastructure that taxpayers usually don't resent, like hospitals, schools, transport, defence, research and legal aid.

The rich use public services, too. In his 2024 book on Australian inequality, *Battlers and Billionaires*, Andrew Leigh MP points out that 'while higher income people are lighter users of the income support system, they tend to be heavier users of other public services, including universities, roads and airports'. Even the huge tech giants, supposed archetypes of entrepreneurial free-marketism, have relied heavily on early state funding. The economist Mariana Mazzucato has pointed out that 'every major technological change in recent years traces most of its funding back to the state'. It's one of the greatest public hoodwinks of all time that Apple, Tesla and Google are rugged capitalist innovations when in fact all of them relied on government funding at some point in their evolution. The risks are taken on by the state, but the rewards are all privatised.

These companies of course go to extraordinary lengths not to pay the taxpayer back, even via their fair share of basic corporate taxation. The state also mops up the fallout – the multi-billionaire family behind Walmart in the US pays its employees so little that many rely on food stamps and Medicaid. Not only does the media more frenziedly pursue the odd lapse of individual judgement, but the Australian Tax Office also spends far more pursuing minor cases of evasion than large-scale ones. When it comes to billions of dollars of unpaid corporate tax, does the media headline scream 'our taxes paid for THIS' above a picture of a superyacht? It seems the larger and more egregious the white-collar crime, the more we're accustomed to tolerating it.

Some commentators argue that the mere existence of billionaires is a colossal failure of policy. We tolerate wealth of this nature, in part, because our brains are notoriously ill-equipped to grasp huge numbers; we can't fathom the magnitude of difference between a not-that-rich millionaire celebrity and a mind-bogglingly rich billionaire. Translating things into relative pricing, or 'normal money', helps but still doesn't quite get you there. Jeff Bezos' seemingly extravagant US$47 million wedding represented only 0.02 per cent of his net worth. That would be the equivalent of an average Australian (based on an average net worth of $1.46 million) spending a measly $292 on their wedding. Business Insider worked out that the average billionaire can easily afford to withdraw and spend 4 per cent of their net worth, or around US$80 million, in a given year. A little rundown of relative costs posited that a trip to Bali for a week would be like the average American buying a $1 chocolate bar, and a down payment on a typically priced house would be the equivalent of $35 for an Average Jane.

We're not nearly as furious as we could be at the regulatory failures that have normalised all this. And as noble as any philanthropic (and tax-deductible) gestures may seem, even endowments of millions are still only a drop in the ocean compared with the taxes the megarich are avoiding. According to the Tax Justice Network, tax evasion by corporations and wealthy individuals costs the world half a trillion USD a year. Australia is one of the 'hurtful eight' OECD countries who keep thwarting a global framework that would crack down on these havens (the catchily named *Intergovernmental Negotiations for UN Framework Convention on International Tax Cooperation* – another fabulous place to hide the keys to the revolution).

IT'S ALL TOO easy to turn away from dull, confusing things when we're endlessly distracted. So many aspects of our daily lives in liberal democracies are designed to deflect us from grim reality or make us believe that our leaders can't act for us anyway. Not only are we working longer hours at our day jobs and parenting our children and pets more intensively than any other generation has done; we're also constantly diverted by online formats that are deliberately crafted to monopolise our attention. The few media outlets without paywalls, or content producers on our Instagram feeds, really have to hook us to stop us scrolling on to the next thing. Tax is not that thing.

There's plenty of wilful blindness in the mix, too, particularly when it comes to saving money. Even when I worked at the progressive think tank and spouted off about social justice, at home I almost daily took cheap, next-day delivery of Amazon packages that sported the telltale return address in Luxembourg. Like many, I was happily living in a state of cognitive dissonance – completely conscious of the issues involved but still putting my wallet and convenience first. And this sort of consumer decision-making is a self-reinforcing cycle: as we get increasingly squeezed by inflation and interest rate rises, as more and more public services are cut and wages stagnate, the more something being cheap is important to us. So, we end up in acts of what Marxists would call the most spectacularly self-defeating false consciousness – buying cheap sweatshirts with *Monte Carlo* embroidered on them from the corporations that are hiding out there tax-free and swindling us out of the public services we need. The more inequitable our society has become, the more we seem to want a stake in these pseudo-luxury items that fetishise extreme wealth and bear absolutely no resemblance to the lives we lead. If a bunch of billionaires and a dazed Katy Perry orbiting Earth for no reason wasn't our 'let them eat cake moment', perhaps nothing will be.

We're also regularly threatened away from the conversation. The standard response to any gentle proposition regarding tax reform, or even any attempt to enforce basic tax *compliance*, goes something like this: *if you raise taxes on capital, on the huge financial transactions in the city, the country's fortune makers will go away and take their money elsewhere.* While there's truth in the idea that loopholes can be exploited if there isn't international co-operation, the idea that all the wealth creators will up and leave is demonstrably untrue. The LSE Inequalities Lab in the UK found that most of the super-rich folk they interviewed had absolutely no desire to leave their homes and family networks for tax havens or lower tax nations, and they were also quite concerned about the stigma and upheaval involved in doing so.

For the online marketplaces and tech behemoths, the threat is simple, untrue and extremely effective: if you come for us demanding more tax, we'll have to put up prices, and that will only hurt you. Leave us alone, and we'll get wealthy and stimulate the country's economy, and then you too will thrive.

AND WE'RE BACK to trickle-down. Nobel Prize–winning economist Joseph E Stiglitz joins the former Pope in whacking this persistent mole:

> As we've seen, higher inequality has not led to more growth, and most Americans have actually seen their incomes sink or stagnate. What America has been experiencing in recent years is the opposite of trickle-down economics: the riches accruing to the top have come at the expense of those down below.

A rising tide hasn't lifted all boats – it's just enabled some to invest in even bigger boats and buy their way out of contributing to the upkeep of the harbour. To more accurately represent the gulf between rich and poor in Australia in this picture, we'd have to say that some don't even have the benefit of boats. They're treading filthy water as the cruise ships float by.

Yet the more dire the situation has become, the more we've lost confidence in our leaders – even the ones who are trying to help overturn these paradigms. After the global financial crisis of 2007–09, even the Queen was asking tough questions of the economists who'd failed to predict it. Our trust in institutions has been calculatedly eroded: thanks to some powerful public messaging and scapegoating, every public servant, academic and politician was chucked together in the same amorphous, villainous package of 'elites' who'd trashed the economy, sent jobs offshore and caused a crashing decline in living standards. Why trust the government to take your money and redistribute it?

The flames of populist anti-elite, anti-government sentiment have of course been fanned by algorithmically made-to-measure misinformation on social media. In 2024, the Department of Home Affairs released the *Strengthening Australian Democracy* agenda, which highlighted that younger people and those struggling financially were less likely to trust the government. And those who are struggling financially are, naturally, the ones who stand to gain or lose the most from any policy decisions regarding tax reform.

And the final, fatal twist? Some aspects of large-scale tax reform are legitimately a bit complicated. It isn't immediately simple to reform tax policy in terms of tax havens and major wealth taxes, especially in a globalised economy. Any type of significant haven reform really needs buy-in from all others in our networked economy. Four G20 ministers came together to propose a meagre 2 per cent wealth tax on billionaires in 2024. But without the others following suit, major accountancy firms will simply negotiate more workarounds for their clients.

That's not to say it shouldn't be done – many visionary policy changes we now accept as part of the furniture were once off-puttingly labyrinthine tasks – but that it's easy for national governments to simply shrug and point to the web of international economic relationships, saying: 'No one else is doing it, so what's the point starting here?' This is where international agreement comes in, but we're back to the deeply unsexy UN consensus panel process.

One could have supposed that the leaking of the Panama, Paradise and then Pandora papers might have knocked the whole tax havens thing on the head, but somehow a very good job was done of making these complex shell companies and offshore trusts seem like a necessary (and, crucially, quite legal) evil: a price for doing business and one that was far too complicated to try to unravel. With major accountancy firms making huge sums from serving up a 'Double Dutch with a side of Irish', and other fabulous tax-avoidance concoctions, it wasn't just the owners of the trusts who had something to lose if this racket was broken up. This scam implicates Australia, too. In 2023, an international report revealed that Australians alone keep $370 billion in offshore tax havens, depriving the Treasury of $11 billion in tax revenue. In his regularly updated book, *Tax Secrets of the Rich*, Kerry Packer's former accountant boasts of the many ways in which a high-net-worth individual can dodge and thwart what he describes as the 'game' of the ATO's 'subjective' and random rules.

It's a textbook vicious cycle. Boredom, lack of knowledge, misinformation, complexity and apathy feed one another and only deepen our antipathy towards the institutions that have the power to change the game. What we're really lacking is some sort of clear moral vision about what tax is and should (and could) be. Inequality is a moral issue, and too often economic debates are starved of the ethical ideas and language that should underpin them. What, and how much, we tax matters. Economic theories reflect what we value and what we regulate – they're not some impossible-to-govern market force we must submit to. A staggering 40 per cent of First Nations people in Australia survive without two or more essentials (housing, clean water or food) required for an adequate standard of living. We tolerate this injustice, just as we tolerate the superyachts in Darling Harbour.

Perhaps Joel will never develop an independent passion for tax reform. But our democratic representatives are still free to step ahead of his demand for it. While the history books aren't exactly heaving with examples of major, non-popular, politician-led movements for change, there have been a few: John Howard's gun amnesty, the smoking ban, seatbelts. On the surface, these are safety policies and thus lie in a different category of intervention, but is inequality really so different? Poverty is a condition that leave its sufferers in precarious and unsafe situations; there's a reason housing, clean water and food are termed 'essentials'.

The Norwegian Prime Minister Jonas Gahr Støre, one of three European leaders to implement a wealth tax, spoke boldly to the ultra-rich who threatened an exodus afterwards: 'When you've made your wealth in Norway, put your kids in school, benefited from the healthcare system, driven on the roads and reaped the rewards of its research, it's a breach of the social contract.' The Welsh Government recently reformed its woefully regressive council tax, even in the face of focus groups that didn't fully understand the issues or call for their implementation. Housing is much harder to hide than income and is a good proxy for it. Commentators such as Alan Kohler have called to – at the very least – limit negative gearing to new builds and to cut capital gains discounts to 25 per cent. But will Albanese and Chalmers be brave enough to make larger paradigmatic changes than these, even if no one asks them to?

FIFTEEN YEARS AGO, my colleagues and I featured a debate about the new 'Robin Hood Tax Campaign' in our public program of events. 'It's a simple and beautiful idea that has found its time,' said the actor Bill Nighy. He joined *Four Weddings and a Funeral* director Richard Curtis and celebrated economist Jeffrey Sachs to launch the campaign run by a coalition of over fifty major charities, including Comic Relief, Christian Aid and UNICEF.

The financial crisis still felt recent then, and there was an excited, restless energy in the room. A simple 0.005–.05 per cent Tobin-style tax on major bank-to-bank transactions was pitched as the single quickest, most painless way to raise billions for poverty relief and climate action. The FTT (financial transaction tax) had some critics, but one thousand G20 economists penned a letter of support, and it seemed we were on the precipice of change.

In the process of writing this piece, I tried to find out what happened to the Robin Hood tax. It turns out the idea was kicked around for many years, and the latest update I could find was from 2023. The European Commission said there was 'little expectation that any proposal would be agreed in the short term'. The website is now archived and redirects to a hopeful new campaign – one that promises to 'Make Polluters Pay'.

Abi Stephenson is a writer who has published in *The Guardian*, *Aeon*, *The Monthly* and *Australian Book Review* and is a curator of ideas-led events, broadcasts, festivals and award-winning animations. For more than a decade, she programmed and produced the Royal Society of Arts' books and ideas events in London and was the editor and producer of the Webby-winning RSA Animates and RSA Shorts.

Olivia De Zilva

This woman's work

Life seemed easier – in the Tampon ads – like go roller-skating *or* scale
a mountain with a heavy flow – but she wakes up straight to the train –
the plastic smile of productivity memes paywaving through the day – it's
cringe to be a girlboss it's oppressive to gatekeep it's (un)trauma informed
to gaslight – *so* – how does the modern woman make it in this world(?)
www.seek.com jobs for gals who brunch (love a spicy marg) pilates away
the pain and who can clickity clack deadlines by 12 pm her *Momager*
gave up her *Sugar Daddy* stopped paying – if Jimmy Barnes was the
working class man in slutty cut offs and hard yakka who is 'she' – Insta
says: 'on' – *so here's what I eat in a day* – a prune, ginger shot TikTok lunch
cheat day dinner (no carbs!) tucked in her spreadsheets she does it again
(and again) (and again) (and again) (and again) Logs into Reddit 'why
can't I get it together' 'what's my kibbe style' 'what constitutes a "girl
dinner"' 'how can I join a run club when I have a FUPA (no judgement
pls)' – glides through the office in a pair of worn down kitten heels
gets an ugly dog for companionship names it syllabically similar to an
ex-boyfriend the last glass of pinot is always and delectably *hers* this
paycheque is lacking a few 00s on R U OK? Day someone says they hope
she finds someone her phone is confiscated because Hinge notifications
disrupted the team meeting *why is it so hard* to be forever skinny fat/a
gemini & cancer rising/pear shaped/some asshole's daughter/to have an
aura/mysterious/a kleptomaniac/an empath/a girl (but not yet a woman)
asks ChatGPT how to make money (quick) how to get over heartbreak
(without thinking about it) book a tour for me with likeminded singles
away from a war zone there is no cure for wellness not in the self-help
books or succubus chic she wishes she started a funny Twitter account
with hot takes or a TikTok where she cuts up outfits for views or became

a YouTube chef that makes homely meals for her family not from a
packet there are endless opportunities for women's work – netball coach
or cleaning lady or She-E-O or marketing manager or ferris Wheel
operator – where does it start or end? Ping ponging her head between
billboards – a soap made out of bathwater is not for the gals – but a
LV sports bra is akin to the suffragettes – the weight of the world
rests on her unshaved shoulders – this woman's work – algorithmises
in her soft hands – Ozempic prescriptions SKIMS tummy tuck pants
makeup tutorials for adults who only know how to use face paint
HELLOFRESH 20% off vouchers a new gym a new you <3 Lena
Dunham's latest think piece videos of dogs being put down (so you can
feel again) why this one hack can remove the fat from between your
thighs a cure for chub rub a wellness retreat in Ubud Taylor Swift happy
moments jeans to match your genes Goodreads recommendations to get
you back on track it's that easy

Olivia De Zilva is a writer based in Kaurna Yerta (Adelaide). Her novel *Plastic Budgie* was released in July 2025 by Pink Shorts Press. Her novella *Eggshell* was released by Spineless Wonders in November 2025. Her fiction and essays have appeared in *The Guardian, SBS, The Saturday Paper, Mascara Literary Review* and many other publications. Olivia's writing has been shortlisted for the Richell Prize, the Kat Muscat Fellowship and the Deborah Cass Prize, and she was recently the inaugural winner of the AAWP Novella Prize.

NON-FICTION

Back to the future

The economics of time and space

Rick Morton

I RETURN, AGAIN and again, to the future.

This was not always a place available to me, even when I tried to dream it into being. It simply did not obey the laws of my existence: the impoverishment of my childhood, the precarity of my early adulthood, the way the first authored so much of the second.

In my late teens and early twenties, even as I worked full time, I lurched from one financial crisis to the next. I crashed more than one barely roadworthy car, slept in a hire car when I became temporarily homeless – at a cost that ate up most of my pay – and paid bills and debts late, or not at all, until the missed payment fees became their own longstanding category of expense, eternally on the ledger.

The cost of doing business, I reasoned. Each day demanded that I rob from myself. A future version of myself, to be exact. I would chip away at that guy's potential, shrink him, until the present was survivable, if not totally bearable.

As lonely as this existence could be, I was not, in fact, alone. My family and I bore the reciprocal costs of this shared moment-to-moment rock-hopping. Our dues were paid into the same bucket, and from the same bucket did we draw our occasional minor victories and common defeats.

In collectivist cultures and some – though, I stress, not all – subsets of the poor, there's a duality of community: they are responsible for you and, in return, you for them. As much as my single mother had worked to set me free, it was probationary.

So, I worked, for myself and my mum and my much younger sister. And occasionally my older brother. And they worked, in return, for all of us, reinforcing the spokes in the wheel of our family. Sometimes we also worked against one another, as spokes are wont to do.

I've seen the best and worst of this phenomenon. In Steinbeck's great novel *The Grapes of Wrath*, there's a moment, long into the Joad family's dust-bowl march for work and food, that has scored my brain. The Joads have arrived on some conglomerate farm operation, starving and depleted like the Oklahoma they left behind, and must work picking peaches before the promise of a pittance with which to feed themselves.

But how to work with broken bodies and a hunger that scratches at bone? The company farm has a general store – inflated prices, naturally; you want it cheaper, you go into town and waste your own gas – where the pathetic workers can get credit for work done before being paid proper.

Ma Joad takes her family's slip for $1 into the store and can barely afford the basics. Later, she begs for some sugar. The clerk, filled with shame at the work he does – he's just another mouth trying to feed more mouths – eventually relents and chucks in a dime of his own to be repaid when the Joads come back. As she goes to leave, Ma turns and offers her hard-won insight. 'Thanks to you, I'm learnin' one thing good. Learnin' it all a time, ever' day. If you're in trouble or hurt or need – go to poor people. They're the only ones that'll help – the only ones,' she says.

This is not to suggest every poor person everywhere will be helpful. Only that of those who do help, they're always poor. Ma Joad knew this as an essential truth. But she also knew that scarcity breeds contempt.

Princeton sociology professor Matthew Desmond spent years speaking with America's underclass and the slumlords who rent to, and then evict, them. In his book that followed, naturally called *Evicted* (2016), Desmond builds on powerful observations from researchers who came before him about the ability of the down-and-out to close the fire door on others just like them.

Desmond found this instinct particularly true when considering the residents of trailer parks – mostly but not entirely white – who were all desperate to hold on to a patch of their own peace. 'Trailer park residents rarely raised a fuss about a neighbor's eviction, whether that person was a known drug addict or not,' he writes. 'Evictions were deserved, understood to be the outcome of individual failure. They "helped get rid of the riffraff," some said. No one thought the poor more undeserving than the poor themselves.'

Any one person or family had to see injustice in order to change it, but they also had to believe in their collective capacity to change it. And that belief must arise from some notion of a future. 'For poor people, this required identifying with the oppressed, and counting yourself among them – which was something most trailer park residents were absolutely unwilling to do,' he writes.

In Australia, and especially my home state of Queensland, we're awash with this inward contempt thrust outward. It's a contempt that makes it easy to judge the poor and the broke alike for the perceived deficiencies of character that have led to their sorry little lives and are, in turn, a necessary part of the matrix of injustice that hurts us: the good ones who've had sorry little lives thrust upon them.

The upshot of this displaced aggression is that the future – any future – is for those with the means to conjure it. So, it makes perfect sense to shovel solace into the present as best you can. Sometimes this looks like a new television set thanks to a sudden windfall or buying the kids some 'superfluous' toy that actually disguises a sliver of the penury in which they live. For others, it's tobacco and alcohol, or gambling, which run the gamut from mindless distraction to full-blown addictions. These little wins mean a lot in the present, but they're not structural. And they're never enough to bet on the future.

Meanwhile, possible lives collapse into the only one permitted. Options evaporate. Paths no longer fork.

THAT I WAS, am, bad with money is not a revelation. But sometimes money is bad with us. It has strange physical and psychic properties.

I've often told friends and lovers that I have a gambler's brain – there's no version of the marshmallow experiment where I'm not found with the first one stuffed in my mouth by the time the researcher returns with the second. But one day, I began to see a week ahead and then a month and then a few years. The future emerged as if from a heavy, parting fog.

All the therapy in the world could not have delivered this to me. It was my income and only my income. As I scratched my way into the middle class – you can still see the claw marks on a Volkswagen dealership in Canberra – I bought nice pots and pans and started cooking, trying new recipes and discovering, at the age of thirty-three, exotic (to me) sauces and pastes. Things like kecap manis and gochujang. More time passed, and I started exercising and then learning French. I worked more and more, but there was still so much time to think about matters of passion and dedication.

Time that had never been there before, like energy locked away in the atom, until it was released by some accident of physics.

Money.

When I handed in the manuscript for the extended essay *On Money* in 2020, the very kind and whip-smart publisher wondered whether my riff on Einstein's theory of general relativity and the nature of space and time was distracting from the point of the work. I pushed back, politely: it *was* the point.

Five years later, as I return to the subject, I'm even surer of this fact.

Money warps time and space. The more wealth you have, the more time and space you get to enjoy, quite literally. Having strip mined most of the wealth possible for a single person to have, the world's centibillionaires have turned their insatiable appetites from legacy to actual longevity. To live forever, or at least until they're 150, seems to be the current hope, the new frontier of excess. Some want their bodies to go the distance; others, like Mark Zuckerberg, seem content to move to a digital universe where audiences never die and advertisers can target these people, who surely now wish they were dead, with upgrade tiers for trees or the terrifying simulacra of joy.

This is an extreme demonstration of money's power to spawn options. Many people want only for the chance at a decent life: for housing, food and rest.

Without money, we're forced into narrower and narrower corridors. We live more harshly, worry more constantly and die earlier. There are good stresses and bad stresses; the kinds poverty delivers are those that damage the brain. But a billionaire who loves the extreme thrill of doing business will hurt his brain only if he ends up doing too much ketamine.

Having some money, if not the structural support of family or even wealth, has rippled through my own existence like a wave of gravity, shrinking and expanding space and time around me as my good fortune waxes and wanes.

It's mostly good fortune.

And now, as I approach burnout, I find myself wondering what possibilities have been hidden from us by the sickly mode of capitalism.

THE IDEA THAT there's only so much money to go around makes a bastard kind of sense to the poor. If impossible decisions abound in their lives, it must be true of governments, too. Certainly, that's how federal budgets are framed. But beyond impressionism, we know the household budget is not analogous to state budgets in any meaningful way.

A belief in this scarcity, as real as it may feel, is conceptually deformed.

So, when clipped transmissions of a strange, and I thought new, idea called universal basic income (UBI) struck my radar like interstellar rescue messages half a decade ago, I was sceptical. Instantly dismissive, actually.

Money for everyone, even rich people? It made my skin crawl. That's what franking credits and superannuation tax concessions are for! It was hard enough for people at the bottom to live now – and that was with means testing to theoretically keep benefits for those who needed them most.

What I failed to understand, then, as a product of Australia's targeted welfare system, is that I was also a product of the bludgeoning conditionality that's necessary, we're told, to sustain it.

Take one small but illustrative example.

Welfare, per successive Commonwealth governments, should go only to those who need it. So-called working age payments like JobSeeker are for people who cannot find work or who are between jobs. There were 885,000 people on this payment in July 2024. One quarter of these are aged fifty-five to sixty-four and almost 70,000 have been on or below poverty-level payment for more than a decade. Of the total July number, 370,000 had been officially assessed as having a 'partial capacity to work', which means, in common parlance, they have a disability. Many of these are cast-offs from a previous 2012 Labor mission to tighten the screws on the Disability Support Pension, but I digress.

In the official terminology of Australia's social security law, these people are known as 'compellable'. They must be looking for work, or some denuded equivalent of 'activation' – welfare recipients and almonds, it turns out, must be activated – or else have their payments suspended and then cancelled.

Successive governments have performed this policy compulsion for decades now, using an increasingly rococo pyramid scheme of outsourced private 'employment service providers' vested with the power to make a fortune off the backs of welfare recipients. Part of this fortune flows from their ability to suspend government payments if a person refuses to enrol in a training module offered by a company that can also be owned by the job provider.

Nice work if you can get it.

We could explore all of the ways this system acts as a sort of puppy mill for the poor, or the fact of its overarching Targeted Compliance Framework embedded in Australian law being so eye-wateringly complex that the three federal agencies charged with overseeing it – three! – misread half a dozen sections of the legislation for years, cutting hundreds of thousands of people off from payments illegally.

But let's set all that aside.

The Commonwealth spends $17 billion a year on income support for the 885,000 people on JobSeeker and then another $1.3 billion a year just on contracts to private companies to enforce the web of conditions attached to receiving that same income support. It's inefficient even writing it out.

To put this more plainly, we've determined, rhetorically at least, to support people who need financial help and then to blow a lot of unnecessary cash to make their lives worse to qualify them for that help. This gerrymandered system of conditionality costs even more in public service effort: the guy who created the robodebt scheme, an illegal government program that could exist only because of this conditionality, once ran the largest single branch in the entire Commonwealth Government. It had three thousand people dedicated to the soulless craft of compliance. In a project like this, compliance types are frequently trying to justify themselves. And not just themselves, but more of themselves. 'Would that there was money for more compliance,' they cry, 'and we'd save so much money!'

Governments have repeated versions of the mantra that reinforces this system – the right payment to the right person at the right time. Indeed, they've built mini empires in service of it. The *raison d'être* of these imperial land grabs is to make an ever larger, ever more complicated machine do a job that, were it not for ideology, does not need to be done.

All this chicanery because they don't want some povo making art on the government dime.

The appeal of UBI, not fully apparent to me until I almost collapsed mentally from overwork and just wanted to go and make art on that government dime, is that there are no conditions. In its pure form, a UBI is money with no strings attached. No more compliance. No more make-work.

Orthodox objectors to this apparently radical idea tend to assert that recipients will just spend the cash on sex, drugs and gambling. Or, worse, that they will simply give up on a 'job'. Whether by osmosis or direct ideological transmission, that's what this contention boils down to. The gears of capital are greased by cheap labour, of which there's a finite supply. One cannot have the labourers running off the mill site and being happy.

Studies of some inconvenience to this point of view are beginning to emerge, however.

What I find most interesting about the work that's starting to crystallise on UBI and similar programs is not so much that people choose to continue working in addition to receiving a basic, survivable income – that always seemed obvious to me – but that in almost every study, one of the benefits that accrues is, quite literally, a future.

In Finland, where a trial was branded an actual and political failure, the results from an unconditional UBI being provided to two thousand randomly chosen, initially unemployed people nevertheless revealed important insights. Early results showed no boost in employment, which helped torpedo the project because permission for the experiment flowed from testing whether it could help solve problems of unemployment for the state. Still, the final results revealed there was actually a small increase in employment. More credibly, to me, the study also significantly improved multiple measures of recipients' wellbeing. McKinsey & Company, the corporate undertaker with a reputation for brutality, found that the 'basic income seems to have improved all the major components of life satisfaction'. In particular, 'people receiving the basic income reported better health and lower levels of stress, depression, sadness, and loneliness – all major determinants of happiness – than people in the control group,' four of the firm's partners and researchers found. 'Recipients of the basic income also demonstrated more confidence in their cognitive skills, assessing their ability to remember, learn, and concentrate at higher levels than the control group did.'

They felt a higher degree of trust in their own future but also in their fellow citizens and public institutions.

None of this feels especially revelatory to me, but the evidence pops up again and again around the world as more trials and studies get going or conclude, mapping a rising interest in the idea of UBI.

In Ireland, a trial of a basic income for artists has now been made permanent after showing remarkable early results: while income from non-arts work reduced by about €280 per month, the increase in money earnt from artistic endeavours was nearly double that at €500.

This data shows, of course, that artists were able to spend more time in the field of their talents than working casual shifts in a café or on a bike delivering takeaway for a grim fee. Naturally, this shift in the *type* of work, from wages to self-employment, should counter the antipathy towards UBI from old capital.

It's not necessarily that people will stop working – in study after study, there's either no observable change in employment (but an increase in wellbeing, which saves government money in other ways) or a jump in employment. No, what bothers some critics is that it's not the right kind of work for the 'propulsive logic' of capitalism, as the South African writer Hein Marais describes it. The factories will not run on dreamers with easels and a few bucks. And how can global capital maintain its momentum if the workers with bad jobs in bad places are given the chance to plan for a better future?

One of the most rigorous research efforts, which began in 2016 and is ongoing, involves a three-group UBI in Kenya where every adult in every house in several communities receives a basic income in one of three ways: as a lump sum, as a promise of regular payments over twelve years equal to the lump sum, or as a set of regular payments over two years.

We see similar results to previous studies here. Most people in the Kenya trial are employed in menial farm work, if they're employed at all. So far, over the long-term UBI stream, the number of non-agricultural enterprises has jumped by one quarter while agricultural assets – the price of land, responding to the purchasing power of recipients, but also of small and large livestock – have increased in value by 35 per cent. Crucially, in the long-term stream, while there's a net economic boost in addition to profound wellbeing milestones, there's a significant drop in hours of waged work. *Quelle horreur!* However, this drop is more than outpaced by the increase in hours worked in 'non-agricultural self-employed work'.

Freedom in this instance is created by the sheer fact of money. Nothing else has changed in the lives of these people, in aggregate, other than money. Particularly in the long-term stream, the effect isn't only about money – but the promise of stable income into the future. This promise creates what the economists call 'option value' or, more humanely, the ability to afford to wait. For the right job, the right opportunity. Time fattens, becomes roomy.

In this fashion, then, we can see how this simple arithmetic produces the psychological effects that pop from this study's experimental design. They're particularly interesting because they test something that's hard to verify but every poor person knows to be true. As with the Finnish trial, there was a 'substantial reduction in reports of depression' among those guaranteed to receive the UBI over twelve years. The size of this effect, however, was 'significantly smaller' – though still present – among those who received the same amount of money but as a lump sum, all in one go.

'Perhaps the lump sum recipients feel the weight of the future more heavily, knowing that they have made their bets and have no further cushion to anticipate if those do not pan out,' Abhijit Banerjee and his co-authors wrote in a September 2023 paper examining early results from the experiment. As they go on to observe, the sudden impost of deciding how to spend a windfall to improve a life is actually quite stressful.

In the UK, researchers from four different universities, led by Neil Howard from the University of Bath, published a paper in the *International Journal of Social Determinants of Health and Health Services* in August 2024 describing workshops held with scores of participants in South Tyneside, north-east England. This was the site of a proposed UBI trial in which participants were asked about how such a trial might work and what it might allow.

The responses map neatly onto the academic theory that props up UBI discussions. As Howard and his colleagues note, a stable and ongoing no-strings-attached payment could 'remove the survival-related compulsion that is one of the defining characteristics of life in poverty'. Participants recapitulated my own experience in their imagined 'counterfactual world of sufficiency'.

'Maybe the reason why we find it difficult to eat healthy or to exercise or to find the things that we enjoy doing is partly because our brains are changed because of the stress that we're under,' one woman, in Generation Y, said. 'So I wonder whether actually just having a different system where we have that money would mean we were under less stress and have more chance.'

These findings alone should be enough to recommend the idea as deserving of some serious inquiry.

It may yet turn out that the features we expect do not emerge at scale, or that governments pervert the idea during implementation, as is their custom. Distance between idea and reality represents a weakness ripe for exploitation. One gets the sense, for example, that the concept of UBI has become a stalking horse for the interests of the artificial intelligence bro-tosphere – think the Nerd Reich's Elon Musk or OpenAI's dark-timeline Ratatouille, Sam Altman – that seek to destroy the environment, the climate and perhaps even humanity itself with the promise of the most vast, and vastly inept, technological change since the flammable blimp.

It's not philanthropy that guides their hearts but self-interest.

Even when it doesn't work as advertised, as we have seen, the disruptive effect of AI technology and its infrastructure is so extreme that even the most powerful men in the world feel the need to shield it with utopian overlays. AI may render two thirds of human jobs obsolete in the near future, but don't worry about it, they say, because everyone will have a liveable wage with our advocacy. Altman and Musk aren't objectors to UBI, but they are in search of a social licence for their destructive tech fever dreams.

Don't fall for the artifice of the argument. People want to work. And that includes work that's not itemised or valued by capital. A UBI can be brought into being without laying waste to these options but in addition to them so that freedom to choose might actually mean something.

I'D MOVED TO Paris for a year by the time I started writing this piece. It was the result of my same old impulses in the face of massive overwhelm, now buttressed by middle-class things like savings. Even after buying a house in my country Queensland hometown for my mother and me, I was saving. Possibly because I was working four different jobs and had become a hermit.

My trip to France was – is – expensive and, at the age of thirty-eight, the most decadent thing I've ever done. I've taken unpaid leave and continue to pay the mortgage, but I've come here to write the novel I've always tried yet failed to write. Within a week of arriving, however, I realised my savings would not be enough. I kept working. A new kind of money stress crawled between me and the work I really wanted to be doing. All things considered, you'd rather have this stress than the alternative, but still I felt my thoughts collapsing as my head jammed up.

Then, three months in, I won the Prime Minister's Literary Award for Non-Fiction, which comes with a tax-free $80,000 prize. Characters and concepts for my novel, once forced out of the expensive real estate of my mind, began to gather again.

I could see their future so clearly.

Rick Morton is an author and reporter currently living in Paris.

Mark O'Flynn

Conditions of Entry

Thirty lines max, it says.
Only twenty-nine left
as some wag might have quipped
but who's counting?
All bags must be opened for inspection.
All poems disassembled and unpacked
so as to demonstrate nothing
untoward lurking in the subtext.
No shirt no service.
You, the poet, are responsible for your
own baggage and semantic flaws.
Any rhyme, oblique or otherwise
must be accompanied by a medical
certificate, plus a notice of authenticity
from a registered metre dealer.
Irony will not be subsidised.
Metonymy and waffling will lead
to immediate disqualification.
Please turn your phone to airport mode.
Any attempt to obfuscate will be regarded
as mickey-mousing and relegated to
the back seat of unflattering ambiguity.
Do not gild the lilac lily, Larry.
Neither will alliteration nor alteration be
allowed after submissions close.
No correspondence will be entered into.
Keep your name to yourself.
No time off for good behaviour.
Absolutely no
refunds.

Mark O'Flynn has published several collections of poetry as well as two collections of short stories, *White Light* (Spineless Wonders, 2013) and *Dental Tourism* (Puncher & Wattmann, 2020). His novels include *The Last Days of Ava Langdon* (UQP, 2016), *Grassdogs* (HarperCollins, 2006) and *The Forgotten World* (HarperCollins, 2013).

NON-FICTION

Pay writers like politicians

Rethinking Australia's literary funding

Catriona Menzies-Pike

IN THE EARLIEST days of the Australia Council for the Arts, before the passage of the Australia Council Act in 1975, members of the fledgling Literature Board fielded radical proposals about how the federal government could support the development of a national literature. Thomas Shapcott, in a 2004 memoir of his time on the board, recalls that a guaranteed minimum income scheme for writers was on the table in those first meetings in 1973, though it didn't go far. Even more startling were the calculations around major fellowships: three-year grants awarded by the Literature Board to writers of talent and reputation. Shapcott as well as Richard Hall, who was Gough Whitlam's private secretary prior to the 1972 election, made the case for increasing the annual stipend of $4,000 offered by the Commonwealth Literary Fund (CLF) to $9,000. Their reasoning seized my attention. 'Our argument,' he writes, 'was that $9,000 represented both a middle-range journalist's salary, and was also equivalent to that payable to backbenchers in federal parliament. We proposed that our writers were worth at least as much as a parliamentary drone.'

The audacity of this proposal made me gasp, as did the recklessness of the phrasing. I do believe that writers are as valuable to the flourishing of our democracy as politicians, but I've become so thoroughly assimilated to the paternalistic austerity of Australian cultural funding, to the abysmally low rates of pay that are now the standard for writers, that I wouldn't dare to suggest they get paid hundreds of thousands of dollars a year. Now, our benchmarks are the poverty line and the minimum wage. Our expectations for government support of writers are modest. Be reasonable, we're advised. Be realistic.

When we talk about Australian books and writers today, we often find ourselves talking about money. Like patients with chronic illness, we've become adept at enumerating the symptoms of our malaise. We talk about broke writers and broke publishers and broke editors. Is anyone making any money? We talk about the cost of books and the cost of paper. We talk about writers' incomes and the salaries of publishing staff. We talk about the cost of housing and university redundancies. There simply isn't enough grant funding to go around. We talk about who can't afford to write. We talk about the indie publishers selling out to multinationals because the margins are too tight. We talk about the market – the market for Australian literature that's so small, even a prize-winning bestseller doesn't bring financial security to its author. The market can't be trusted with our national literature – unless what we want is self-published erotic fiction, which is apparently where the money lies. We talk about the obscenity of wealthy tech corporations shitting on copyright. If tech companies won't pay writers, who else will?

Even when we're not talking about money – when we're talking about our hopes for a national literature, or whose stories should be told, when we're talking about easy reading, or books that infantilise their readers, or how to safeguard freedom of expression, or the moral principles at stake in wholesale breach of copyright – our conversations are caveated and curtailed by the money question. At our most ambitious, we talk about how to pay writers a living wage.

Little wonder Shapcott and Hall's vision – which was smothered by inflation, the dismissal of the Whitlam government, the election of Malcolm Fraser – now seems so remote. The major fellowships were 'almost instantly frozen'. What began, Shapcott writes, 'as equivalent to a federal parliamentary backbencher's salary has ended up being much less than that same backbencher's tax-free allowances'. As I write this essay, the base salary for a backbencher in the Australian Parliament is $239,270. The average annual income for an Australian writer – well, you know this already. The 2022 National Survey of Australian Book Authors found that Australian writers earn on average $18,200 each year from their creative work.

FEDERAL FUNDING FOR literature has declined in both real and relative terms since the early days of the Australia Council, with policy settings calibrated to the needs of our comrades in the performing arts. The trend, broadly, has been that Coalition governments have slashed or repurposed arts funding, sometimes singling out funding for literature, as when George Brandis borrowed $6 million from the Australia Council to set up the Book Council of Australia a decade ago. Labor governments have failed to restore funding to earlier levels. In an op-ed written to greet the launch of Writing Australia, *Meanjin* Editor Esther Anatolitis summed it up: 'Over the last decade, federal funding for literature has dropped roughly 43% in real terms, even as writers' incomes have stagnated below the poverty line and threats to their livelihoods have proliferated.'

This long-term, chronic underfunding of the Australian literary sector is one of the reasons the launch of a new federal entity charged with supporting Australian literature was so closely watched. Writing Australia was legislated into being via the Creative Australia Act 2023 and was the final chip of Labor's 2023 national cultural policy, *Revive*, to be slotted into place. At the launch in July 2025, Minister for the Arts Tony Burke announced that Writing Australia would receive $26 million in new funding over three years, on top of the existing $7.8 million invested annually in literature.

Yet the signals being sent do not suggest that drastic changes to the way Australian literature will be funded are en route. Writing Australia will be led by the well-regarded Wenona Byrne, formerly head of literature at Creative Australia, and its advisory council has been populated with experienced industry leaders, not one of whom could be classified as a renegade. These steady hands will be required to cultivate audiences for Australian books and to steer Writing Australia through turbulence generated by the underfunding of literature, the prevalence of large language models and the pressures of global publishing.

In early 2025, Creative Australia squandered the confidence of artists in the arms-length funding process when, under political pressure, they rescinded the appointment of Khaled Sabsabi and Michael Dagostino as Australian representatives to the Venice Biennale before reinstating them months later. Writing Australia must convince writers that their grants will not be subject to political interference and that their freedom of speech will be defended. Even though, in late 2025, the Attorney-General ruled out the Productivity Commission's recommendation that a loophole be created in local copyright law for the purposes of training large language models, Australian writers are still vulnerable to the predations of international tech firms. Writing Australia must continue to defend the right of artists to make a living from their work. These are challenges that have taken on new dimensions since the passage of the Creative Australia Act; the territory delineated by AI is evolving rapidly, making redundant long-held policy assumptions, especially with regard to copyright. A renegade or two might help Writing Australia persuade writers it can keep up with the pace of change.

In the midst of all this, no one is flying any kites about writers getting paid like parliamentarians or even like their staffers, and everyone is curious about how this new funding will be invested. Any optimism that may have been sparked by the launch of Writing Australia was quickly dampened by Melbourne University Publishing's (MUP) announcement in September last year that it intended to close down *Meanjin*. The decision, according to MUP, was made on financial grounds, a claim that was greeted with some incredulity within the industry. Compared with most literary organisations, *Meanjin* was in rude health. If *Meanjin*'s books weren't robust, how could anyone else survive? This closure is a stark reminder of the precarity of Australia's literary organisations, who are all one 'purely financial' decision away from shutdown. The infrastructure of our literature is stretched thin, and conditions are not promising for new journals seeking to foster emerging generations of writers and readers.

FOR ALL THAT the landscape of writing and publishing is shifting, federal arts funding has been distributed to writers in more or less the same way for decades – that is, either directly, via grants, fellowship schemes and the like, or indirectly, via publishers, literary magazines such as *Griffith Review* and *Meanjin*, and other organisations who pay writers fees and advances. Funding panels are charged with taking a whole-of-industry approach, especially when making multi-year organisational funding decisions, but the process largely turns around writers and organisations. Resources for sector-development initiatives have been scarce.

When writers apply for individual grant funding, they propose a system of payment for their work. This might be a flat stipend or a day rate tallied to MEAA guidelines. Grant applicants are encouraged to submit budgets that reflect the actual work they will devote to a project and that embody the principle of fair pay for creative labour. What this means in practice is that a chunk of work covered by grant funding might be paid at award rates, but those sections of a project not under the grant umbrella will not. Completing a major project can involve hundreds if not thousands of hours of unpaid work that's effectively off the books. In her 2022 zine, *Decorum Serves the Rich*, Anwen Crawford breaks down the relationship between her income and her labour for her 2015 contribution to Bloomsbury's 33 ⅓ series, *Live Through This*, and her acclaimed 2021 book, *No Document*. She was awarded $70,000 in grant funding as she was writing the latter: 'I began work in earnest on the writing and research that would become *No Document* in roughly May 2017, and "finished" it about a day before it went to the printer, in February 2021. That's almost four years of work. Now, 70k divided by four years…is not a living income. It's an income subsidy…'

Grant funding, for those lucky enough to receive it, used to represent a more meaningful income subsidy than it does now. Crawford draws on research by Jennifer Mills to show the changing relationship of Australia Council fellowships to the average wage. In the 1970s, senior fellowships for writers were paid at a rate higher than the average wage. Right now, writers can apply for a maximum of $50,000 funding for their projects; the median average wage is close to double that. One of Writing Australia's first investments was a two-year creative fellowship scheme that awards writers $80,000. If this scheme represents progress, it's not much. Only two fellowships were awarded to writers – and $40,000 a year still falls far short of the average wage. The horizon for sector development along these lines is very limited.

Yet in the first decades of Australian federal government support for writers, the model for disbursing government funds to writers was a welfare system: it wasn't grants or fellowships that were paid out, but pensions. The CLF, established in 1908, paid pensions to a select cohort of writers who had fallen on hard times, and sometimes to their widows and descendants. Allocations were made according to literary merit and financial need. Barry Andrews writes, 'once a *de facto* minimum standard of achievement had been reached, the question of poverty became paramount: how poor rather than how good.' In the first year of the program, fourteen out of fifty-one applications were funded. (Incidentally, this is a 27 per cent success rate, higher than the 15–20 per cent rates that Creative Australia advises grant applicants to anticipate.) The CLF supported Henry Kendall's widow, Charlotte, for sixteen years after the poet's death.

It was not until 1939 that the remit of the CLF expanded, in part at the behest of the Fellowship of Australian Writers. Not only did the renovated CLF pay pensions; it was also tasked with educating the public 'to a full appreciation of Australian literature'. It provided assistance to publishers, awarded fellowships to writers and granted funding to magazines. The rhetoric of government literary patronage skewed towards cultivating audiences for Australian literature rather than markets. The CLF supported the publication of new books and the reprinting of significant works of Australian literature, as well as bolstering the teaching of Australian literature in universities. After 1973, when the responsibilities of the CLF were absorbed by the Literature Board of the Australia Council, the board continued to pay pensions to eighteen writers. That scheme was replaced by an Emeritus Fellowship program – and later by the Writers' Emeritus Awards.

The pensions have now long been paid out, and I wouldn't propose reinstating them. The detour into the history of federal literary funding demonstrates that the present model of grants and fellowships is neither timeless nor inevitable. A pension model obviously wouldn't do anything to nurture that generation of Australian writers now coming of age and mired in precarity – but those writers are hardly reaping the benefits of merit-based grants and fellowships either. For most of them, the question of poverty, to borrow Andrews' phrasing, remains paramount.

HOW TO SPEND the Writing Australia windfall? This is the question facing that august council of advisers. If the history of federal literary funding in this country offers some alternatives to over-subscribed grant and fellowship schemes, there are also well-known contemporary prompts. Ireland, for example, finished a pilot basic-income-for-the-arts scheme in 2025. The evaluation of the scheme garnered overwhelmingly positive responses. The basic income eased financial stress for participants, who were chosen at random, once eligibility criteria were met, and allowed them to spend more time on their artistic practice. And in welcome news to policymakers, the scheme generated economic benefits, returning €1.39 for every €1 of public investment. In September 2025, the Irish Government announced that the basic income support scheme for artists would be installed as permanent policy from 2026. In Norway, the federal government purchases a thousand copies of every new title by a Norwegian writer, typically for distribution to public libraries. In Australia, which has five times Norway's population, a writer is understood to have hit the big time if they sell a thousand copies of their book.

Canada provides generous funding to publishers via the Canada Book Fund (CBF), which seeks to foster 'a strong book industry that publishes and markets Canadian-authored books'. Between 2022 and 2023, the CBF granted funding to some 261 publishers. In the 2025–26 budget period, the Canadian federal government was projected to spend CA$37 million on CBF grants and to contribute a further CA$3 million to the fund, in addition to the usual raft of grants for writers. We can see a difference in policy here: Canada prioritises industry development and channels significant funds to publishers. But the starker difference lies in the level of funding. The new funding for Writing Australia is welcome and offers a morale boost for the industry. But is $26 million – spread over three years – enough? Not likely. Can good-faith policy thinking transform Australian literature without adequate funding – or is this where we're stuck?

A boss once warned me against trusting commentators on cultural and higher education policy who were, in his words, rent-seekers. People need to move beyond just asking the government for money, he advised, and come up with some serious policy solutions. Serious. Policy. Solutions. This is the fantasy: we make things better without spending any money. My boss' lesson was that no one will take you seriously if you keep asking for money. Don't make stupid suggestions about bloody writers getting paid ludicrous wages. Make believe that funding levels are not the problem. Don't be ungrateful. Never, ever bite the hand that feeds you. Yet this is exactly what Writing Australia must do: advocate for adequate funding for Australian literature. An additional $8 million a year is not enough. It's true that the archives of Australian literary funding are stuffed with petitions for funding increases, as they are in other, better funded jurisdictions (a recent evaluation of the CBF, which seems astoundingly well-resourced from an Australian perspective, reported stakeholder consensus that a funding increase was overdue).

But innovative cultural policy thinking and round after round of good-faith consultation will not get us out of the cul de sac of austerity. *Rent-seeker* is a term of derogation, but it also captures the objective guiding campaigns for better pay for writers and funding for the literary sector. Writers want to be able to pay their rent. Journals and publishers want to be able to pay their staff and their writers. Everyone is sick of talking about how broke Australian writers are, about how precarity is shaping the novels and poems and plays that are being written, about how abysmal pay keeps our literature white and middle class. If we're resigned to a certain level of impoverishment for writers and arts workers being inevitable, this is where we will remain.

It's a tremendous relief that Writing Australia is operational. But let's not fall into a cycle of servile gratitude, anxious that we might lose any modest gain we've received if we speak up. Writers and literary organisations are, as I've written, often counselled to be realistic in their funding expectations. You can't ask for money that's not there. Bear in mind there isn't much to go around. Perhaps we need to redefine what it means to be realistic. What funding is required for the sector to thrive? Once upon a time, just for a flicker of history, policymakers talked about paying writers like parliamentarians. That won't happen again. But we must set our sights higher than just scraping by.

Catriona Menzies-Pike is a literary critic and editor currently based in British Columbia. She has written widely on Australian literature and critical culture. Between 2015 and 2023, she was the editor of the *Sydney Review of Books*.

NON-FICTION

No small change

Preparing publishing for the future

Alice Grundy

HONESTLY, I WAS a bit shocked. Not only because it was so pointed an accusation but because I hadn't an inkling my friend felt that way. We were drinking orange wine of an evening, talking taboos, when I mentioned something about being middle class. 'But you're upper class,' she replied.

I was surprised – in part because my mum was a teacher and my dad a public servant. Each was the first in their family to get a university degree. We didn't go on fancy holidays, and I paid for my own university education. My income is from labour, not capital. It hadn't occurred to me that I would be anything other than middle class. But this is Australia, and when I later heard Cate Blanchett describe herself as 'middle class' at a Cannes Film Festival press conference, I remembered this interaction.

This is a country that's supposedly shed the class system of the colonial motherland; this is a place founded on mateship and a fair go and collaboration. We don't like tall poppies or people too big for their boots. When a Hollywood movie star, with a personal net worth of around $140 million, who fronts perfume campaigns and appears on red carpets at Cannes, identifies as middle class, they're pilloried, no matter who their parents are. Obviously, I'm no Blanchett. But was I similarly deluded about my place in Australian class networks?

To be fair to my friend, I do have a few tally marks in the 'upper' column. Most of my schooling was private, I speak with a relatively soft Australian accent and I work with books. The third of these three is the biggest giveaway.

As a 2022 industry survey showed, around 50 per cent of respondents – people who also worked in the literary sector – went to private school, compared with only 36.7 per cent of current Australian students. Considering private school numbers are now at an all-time high, the percentage for the total population would have been far lower when these graduates were entering the workforce. Put simply, these figures show the publishing industry is not representative of the Australian public.

But working in publishing isn't just a question of wealth or class. I've been thinking lately about other – broader – inheritances and privileges I've received as an elder millennial. University was expensive but not unaffordable. I started life in a world that was only just beginning to reckon with the catastrophes of human-induced global heating. And I grew up in a house with books and with parents who encouraged reading and intellectual curiosity. The entanglements of publishing, wealth and class are indeed tightly bound, and there's no indication the knots will loosen without some serious interference. Reflecting on these interconnections is uncomfortable given that timing, as well as my upbringing and privilege, has made things possible for me that aren't a possibility for many others. What worries me is that the twin succubae of privilege and exploitation are ready to feed on the next generation of avid readers.

WHEN I WAS around nineteen, my dad bought me a copy of *New Grub Street* by George Gissing. I couldn't read his copy because, so the story goes, he'd underlined all sorts of passages that would have proved too revealing – his particular attention to passages on marriage, career and the life of an intellectual giving away too much. The book is a late-nineteenth-century depiction of the publishing trade in England. It's around twenty years since I last read it, but the thing that's stuck with me most is that each of the characters thinks their life would be better if only they had a little more money. There's the writer living a pauper's existence with barely enough to eat. There's the editor who has a salary but not the life they can see their superiors enjoy. There's the publisher who makes money but looks at the upper classes, noting all the shortfalls in their own life by comparison. Not that a novel should ever be reduced to its moral, but I've never forgotten the principle that looking up leads to despondency. That what might seem like a plentiful life to those with less than you will seem insufficient if your focus remains on what you lack. And that publishing, despite its gentleman's-industry facade, is a grubby business – pun intended. Well, that part I saw firsthand.

I had no intention of working in publishing when I read Gissing's novel; it was thanks to a series of serendipities (read: privileges) that I got my first publishing job. After university, I saved up to travel to France on a working visa for a year. I was happy enough being a waitress and a shop assistant, but my uni tutor's friend connected me with his friend, a literary agent, so I interned for a few months at an impossibly glamorous literary agency. My wage was modest, but since this was France, I enjoyed discounted public transport, and my employer contributed to 'restaurant tickets', effectively covering the cost of most of my lunch each day. Lunch breaks were an hour and a half: plenty of time to get a slice of quiche and wander by the Seine, perhaps have a glass of wine. Co-ordinating my boss' schedule for the Frankfurt Book Fair, buying flowers to put on the desk of a visiting author, recently released from captivity, and eating macarons bought for us by a bestselling client made me think this industry could be a place for me.

Back in Australia, when my visa had run out, I thought I'd stick with publishing. There were fewer political dissidents and pastries: one of the first authors I had to speak with, in my role as a publishing assistant, was an ageing comedian who liked to spew obscenities down the phone at me to get a rise. The vernacular had never sounded so vile. At the age of twenty-four, I wasn't earning enough to start repaying my HECS debt, which included an undergrad degree with honours in the arts – much cheaper before Scott Morrison's Job-Ready Graduates fee hikes – and a graduate certificate in publishing, which I'll return to later. But it was 2008, and you could still get a coffee for $3 (though my Australian employer didn't contribute to my lunch, and there was no discount on public transport). Rents were high in Sydney, much higher than in Paris – but nowhere near the current levels. Obama was in the White House, and it seemed there was a good chance of avoiding the worst effects of climate change.

Even more so than now – given a few small initiatives are aiming to redress the imbalance – the industry was overwhelmingly staffed by white people who'd made similar choices to me: they spent many hours reading and had chosen an industry despite its low wages because they knew that if something were to go seriously wrong in their lives, they had a familial safety net. As long as the industry runs on low wages and high social capital, this situation is likely to continue.

ENOUGH WITH ABSTRACTION: let's talk numbers. Say a person born since the start of the new millennium graduates with a creative writing degree because they like the idea of pursuing a creative career. While people of my generation studied the arts, perhaps with a major in English lit, these days there's an abundance of creative writing graduates. But at the end of that degree, which, thanks to the Job-Ready Graduates program, now costs around $50,000, they might think: *I like reading – how about I work in publishing?* Universities, ever willing to oblige, have publishing and editing qualifications at the ready. There are courses available at many universities now, but there are no more jobs for graduates to move into.

Now, with a HECS debt getting closer to $100,000, our aspiring Gen Z is one of the lucky few to get a job in publishing. Perhaps they have supportive parents, intellectually and financially. Maybe they've been running a YouTube book-review channel since high school or they've worked in a bookshop and interned at a publisher while completing their study (able to work for free rather than pay rent) to differentiate themselves from the two hundred other hopefuls who applied for that publishing assistant job. In this role, they don't earn enough to start paying back their study debt. They're likely in rental stress, trying to live in a capital city on a publishing wage. But after five years of hard work, and by virtue of good negotiating skills, Z makes it to the award wage for senior book editor level 3: just shy of $90,000 per annum. All it took was some postgraduate qualifications, years of industry experience and advocating for the value of their work to arrive at the median Australian wage.

To put this figure into perspective, consider the public service: an employee at level 5 (which is more or less the salary earnt by a public servant editing at a government publisher like the National Library of Australia Press, of which there are one or two positions) would take home the same wage, but with higher superannuation and flex time – a system in which employees can take overtime as leave. Not a senior editor. Not the product of negotiation. The standard salary. Do I hear you protest? *Why doesn't a bookish person just go and work in the public service, then?* Surely, you can imagine yourself in Z's position, though. After all that study – all that grift and grind – wouldn't you want to do the job you've worked for?

If Gissing were to write *New Grub Street* now, the editor would be looking wistfully at an academic – or, at least, they would've until the recent round of chaos in higher education. One of the consequences of so many creative writing degrees is students' proximity to academics who are creative writers, whose research is 'practice-led' and whose novels and other creative publications, even though they require some extra hoop-jumping, can count as academic outputs. Looking around, an editor might turn green when landing upon the perks of academia. If the creative writing graduate got a master's (for which they'd pay course fees) and then a PhD (for which they might receive a scholarship), then wrangled their way into a permanent job, their salary would be around $115,000 from the first year they work with a nice bump from 17 per cent superannuation. When that job includes international travel to conferences, ostensibly paid for as part of the job – how could you not lust after such a career?

But, of course, were Gissing to write such a novel now, he would disabuse his reader of this academic fantasy. Permanent jobs are teasingly rare. Many young academics find themselves working several gigs, given job insecurity and low pay rates. Thanks to some successful union negotiations, permanent staff now have access to a range of enviable conditions; meanwhile, it's increasingly difficult for casual staff to find their way into continuing positions.

One of the practices that allegedly helps with this conversion is getting published – and the de facto arrangement of academia and publishing having birthed a bastard child. Because writing is supposed to be part of academic life – in effect, it's salaried work – academic publishers don't generally pay advances or royalties for the books they publish. What's more, some authors pay for their own image-reproduction fees – or, even better, pay for the book to be made open access, ostensibly with a grant from their employer. An open-access agreement means the publisher makes the work available for free in a digital version with a view to spreading knowledge. In practice, it means the publisher doesn't pay for the content; it's *paid* to produce the content, then it separately sells print books at a profit.

I can imagine an academic publisher bleating at this point: that their market is small, which makes the marginal cost of producing each book so high that they must do whatever they can, as is true for any business, to turn the bottom line from red to black. To which I would reply: Sure, but as long as the motive is profit and the practices extractive, then people will remain indentured to inequitable systems. Models that President Biden legislated in the US at the end of his term, which are just now coming into effect, such as mandating open access for government-funded research, represent one possible way to ensure freer access to research and writing.

MILLENNIALS LIKE ME are accustomed to looking up to previous generations and begrudging their cheaper housing and free education (leaving aside that most who attended universities in the past few decades wouldn't have received a Commonwealth scholarship because far fewer were handed out). But what millennials are yet to reckon with is that those of our generation are in a much better position than those who follow – and not just because of the current cost-of-living crisis. Beyond that, the world today is far more uncertain. A thirty-year mortgage now, if our hypothetical graduate is lucky enough to get the deposit together (most likely thanks to an enormous gift from someone in their family), will collide with an expected rise in temperatures of 2 degrees, which means housing, food and transport will all cost more and become even less accessible.

I knew about global heating when I was growing up. I can still sing the *Captain Planet* theme song. I saw Al Gore's movie at the cinema. I have a KeepCup and buy carbon offsets for my flights. But when I was in my twenties, I didn't feel the clear and present danger of climate catastrophe.

Part of the reason these conversations are so difficult is an unspoken fear that by acknowledging privilege, I accept that whatever position I hold is the product only of my background and not my own hard work. Or it *is* because I happened to be born in a given year and not because of my talent. What this reasoning fails to take into account is that two separate but related things can be true at once. It can be true that I worked hard, including doing plenty of unpaid overtime in my already low-paying job, and that I made some sacrifices. But it can also be true that I wouldn't have been in a position to work those extra hours or have that job at all had it not been for the hours I spent reading as a teenager. I spent those hours reading because I worked only occasionally at the local supermarket and because I was the product of readerly parents who encouraged a life of the mind. It can also be true that a boomer was a visionary and a trailblazer *and* that they didn't work full-time hours while they studied at uni, or that the house they bought by saving hard is now beyond the wildest dreams of their children.

One danger of talking about publishing and money is to speak about the industry as if it's separate from other industries – and from neoliberalism more broadly. The systems of capital, gender and culture are closely enmeshed. Publishing is entangled in the economics of industry, the field of culture and the gender dynamics of broader society. It both replicates and embeds the dysfunctions of society writ large, which means that any corrective would need to be part of bigger system changes that could include increased unionisation, decreasing inequality and greater gender equity.

The benefit of this entanglement, however, is that improvements in publishing can help tug at the threads of other areas of contemporary life. Such improvements don't simply lead to better conditions for editors and writers and publicists and designers but also to more opportunities for people from different backgrounds – and therefore a better chance of publishing a greater range of books. This strengthened diversity, in turn, could help with literacy, accessibility and everything that helps make a world we actually want to live in.

And the reverse is true: improvements in industrial relations for the whole population likewise benefit publishing as well. Once, employers could ask their employees not to discuss their salaries, which put employees at a huge disadvantage. They either didn't know what their peers were earning or had to pretend they didn't. This is no longer the case, but it's still common practice for publishing jobs to be listed without a salary range. Transparency around salaries is a small but important example of how industrial relations improvements across the board could create fairer conditions in publishing.

In the same way, taking seriously the polycrisis of inequality, global heating and increasing conflict will make more kinds of publishing by more people possible into the future. Cultural production is resource-intensive – in time and attention and care – and publishing can be a major contributor to a more equitable, peaceful and temperate world.

It's easy to romanticise the past or to lust after the indulgences of those with more. But the only way to create the publishing industry that so many of us yearn for is through co-operative efforts and increased transparency. This means avoiding the temptation that seduced Gissing's characters – always looking up – and instead looking around at the people who can organise with us to make change. And I'm not talking small change – it's time for the big bucks.

Alice Grundy is an editor, researcher and teacher, with over fifteen years experience working in book publishing.

High life

REBECCA TRAJKOVSKI

My Milkshake Brings All the Boys to the Yacht (2023), acrylic and oil on birch, 93 x 113 cm

If I Have Control Over My Aesthetic I Have Control Over My Life (2022), acrylic on birch, 63 x 43 cm

If Only Life Could Be as Neat as This Ensemble (2022), acrylic on birch, 63 x 43 cm

No. 4 Struggle Street (2024), acrylic on birch, 63 x 83 cm

If You Have This House You Will Be Happy (2025), acrylic on birch, 93 x 113 cm

Same Same but Different (2025), acrylic on birch, 63 x 53 cm

Addicted to Winning (2025), acrylic on birch, 63 x 83 cm

The Board Series 17, No. 2 of 13 (2022), acrylic on board, 45 x 55 cm

The Board Series 20, No. 1 of 3 (2024), acrylic on board, 45 x 55 cm

Turntables over Turnover (2025), acrylic on birch, 53 x 63 cm

Remix of Aspirations (2025), acrylic on birch, 33 x 43 cm

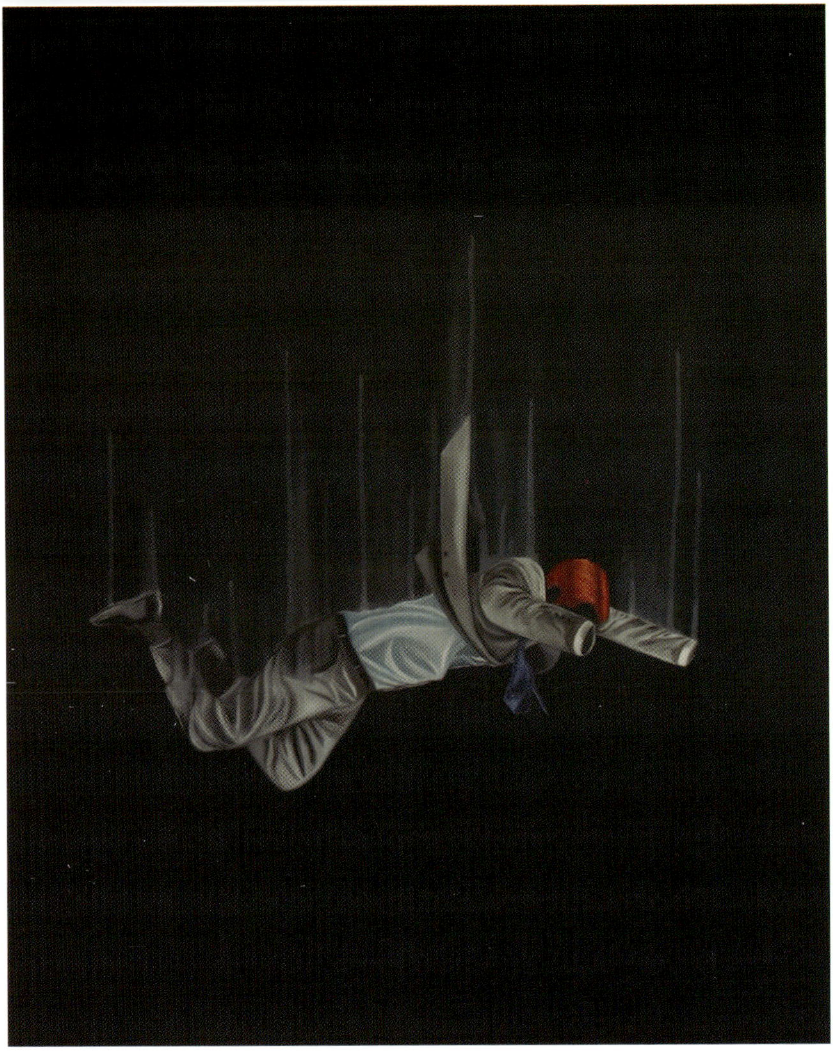

Sink or Swim? (2022), oil on board, 60 x 80 cm

Rebecca Trajkovski is a self-taught artist, a mother and a practising lawyer based in Sydney. She's won the Local Artist Prize in the Georges River Art Prize (2019) and the People's Choice Award in the Law Society's Just Art competition; she was runner-up in the Aspire Gallery Foot Square Art Prize (2019). Her works have been finalists in art prizes including the Blacktown City Art Prize (2019), the Waverley Art Prize (2019), the Georges River Art Prize (2019, 2023), the Lethbridge 20000 Art Award (2020), the Hornsby Art Prize (2022), the BDAS Portrait Prize (2022), the Meroogal Women's Art Prize (2022, 2024) and the Korea Australia Arts Foundation Prize (2022).

Read an interview with Rebecca by scanning the QR code below:

Marjon Mossammaparast

Spirit Mama Bali

for Dessi, Thinker Nails (Ubud)

Spirit Mama Bali wears a wet shirt. Her honey amber coconuts
are unrepentant, and the crescent moon of my nails
is the elegant cummerbund round the waist of her women
who laugh at my money behind my back.

Spirit Mama Bali is in my proverbial strings, shining
with transactable gold. She dangles on the pocket of my lycra pant,
inflates like a balloon the living in my lungs.
My microplastics are iridescent as her spoonbill leaves
catching the morning rain.

Spirit Mama Bali is in my pouch, silver-lined with emptiness.
She scrubs me twice with safety, rolls me in lime
and casts ginger healing on my face.
Lizards are rich and climbing the rails.

Spirit Mama Bali threads my offerings of sovereignty and self.
In her compound houses they stare at my bareness:
no husband, no sons, only the black magic I am paying
for breathwork, reviving my voice box.

Spirit Mama Bali hangs from the thatched roof
conveying the pool and broken road and the open mouths
of wildflowers, eating the bank. She covers her knees
in a boarding room. Julia Roberts flows white in *Namaste*
and floods the rice fields.

Spirit Mama Bali is weeping, flush with exchange,
our gods sitting at the high temples.
The devil is on the pavement
holding his cardboard sign.

Spirit Mama Bali, shooing her biddy fowls. My pores are sweating
the small stuff: yoga legs, charging batteries.
A bike pulls up beside a grandmother stooped by bags.
She hops on; I think of bus shelters far-flung in the 'burbs
a lone trolley unhinged, choking on its dollar.

Marjon Mossammaparast is a poet from Melbourne. Her first collection of poetry, *That Sight* (Cordite Books, 2018), won the 2019 Mary Gilmore Award, was shortlisted for the 2019 Judith Wright Calanthe Award and was commended in the 2018 Anne Elder Award. Her second volume, *And to Ecstasy*, was released in March 2022 through Upswell and was shortlisted for the 2023 Kenneth Slessor Poetry Prize. Her poems have been published widely in a range of Australian journals.

FICTION

The real deal

Miriam Webster

DURING THE FIRST month of my residency I knew hardly anybody in Hanoi. Although I told my friends and family in Australia that I was meeting cool people, making art and experiencing the 'real' Vietnam, I was usually lurking in the Old Quarter with a bunch of expats: some French, American and British men in their fifties with yellow sweat stains bonded to the collars of their business shirts. I made no attempt to start painting, convincing myself that first I needed to find my feet, which took me around the lake and through shopping malls but never to my studio above Thang Long Gallery, not far from where we drank.

It was winter and surprisingly chilly; I had expected it to be warm. During that cool, smoggy month, I spent some of my stipend on a knock-off North Face jacket and thought I understood very little about the world beyond my home.

A friend who'd done a bunch of residencies overseas told me that the best way to immerse yourself in any city was to match with somebody online. You'd go on a few dates, they'd show you all the spots, you'd end up with some local knowledge and, if things went well, a hook-up. Following the logic of much colonial tourism before now, I figured bedding a few locals before the end of your visa was an ideal way to get naturalised. So I downloaded Tinder, telling myself I'd reactivate my old account, when actually the thought of swiping through contenders left me cold. Meanwhile: round after round of beers with Rick, Scotty, Martin and Jerome. The expats didn't even ask where I was from; I simply turned up at the bar one day, and because I was white, I was absorbed into their group.

We didn't have much in common besides English, which we spoke because the men claimed it was neutral. I was younger and the only woman in their party, and I suspected that the expats thought my presence made them more attractive, or at least non-threatening, to the local girls they kept inviting unsuccessfully to drink with us. Sometimes I, too, watched these girls and longed to join them, but before I could make contact, I always lost heart. There was the language barrier, for one thing. But the reluctance spoke to one of my broader pathologies – I was good at beginnings; I rarely saw things through. It didn't matter what I was doing. Something mysterious always happened in the middle that made me want to give it up.

Initially, my inbox swelled with a steady stream of invitations to events and mixers from a person called Suong, the artist liaison for my program, whose name I came to associate with something vaguely sinister, as if this woman – and, by extension, the residency itself – were demanding something I did not know how to give. Perhaps that's why I didn't mind the expats. I didn't feel any pressure to make them like me, and because we were all strangers in a strange land, our acceptance of one another was uncritical. I still dreamt about the crits I'd been subjected to in art school, so I guess I found the ambivalence I felt towards them freeing, in a way.

One night we were drinking and the rain was light and hairy in the streets. I imagined it was falling softly over all of Vietnam, softly falling in the sky-drenched hills north of the city and then mingling greenly with the sea in Ha Long Bay, muffling cries of ecstasy from backpackers on the party boats. Sounds of traffic and a smell particular to Hanoi curled in through the bar's French doors and with a mild shock I realised I was used to it – that, despite myself, I had acclimatised.

I never paid for anything we drank – I assumed because of misplaced chivalry or something – but tonight when beers were set upon the table, Rick from London intercepted mine and sculled it, yelling, 'Taxed!'

I pulled a face.

'What? It's time you settled up.'

As with most alphas, Rick's jokes enacted subtle forms of subjugation. Feeling shamed, I said the next round was on me.

'You're alright,' said Rick. 'We can't expect a backpacker to shout us, even if they are dirt cheap.'

'I'm not a backpacker,' I said.

'You're not?' asked Scotty, a tanned American going through some complicated divorce, looking from me to Rick and back.

'I'm an artist.' I stumbled over the word *artist*, which sounded false. 'I'm on a residency here, developing new work...'

I trailed off. For a moment, the expats watched me silently, maybe even with suspicion. The vibe had shifted. Scotty fumbled with a pack of cigarettes and dropped some on the floor. I bent to help him pick them up, and as I crouched beside his Birkenstock, Rick said, 'You what?'

'It hasn't come up.'

He seemed to be deciding whether to praise or abuse me. Then, suddenly, he clapped me on the back. 'We should be honoured, lads. Fucking Frida Kahlo.'

Martin frowned. 'Is Vietnam rated for its art?'

'What do you mean, Martin?' said Jerome, who was French and considered himself a kind of cultural critic. 'Rated by whom? Based on which standards?'

'I mean...' Martin didn't seem to know what he meant. Then Rick cut in.

'Make any money?'

'Because it's only worth it if it's making someone money?'

'Strap in, lads,' Rick groaned. 'We're about to get a lecture on aesthetics from the fucking Frenchman.'

'Better than a lecture on economics from the fucking English guy,' Jerome retorted. 'Your pathetic countrymen's love of populism landed you in the –'

'Fuck off, mate,' said Rick, waving him away. 'Macron and his precious European Union's no more democratic than –'

'What kind of art do you make?' asked Jerome, cutting his opponent off in turn. This fractious verbal sparring was characteristic of the expats' political conversations, which inevitably became a series of half-uttered phrases, so I could at times deduce, but never quite confirm, which side of politics each one of them was on.

'I paint portraits,' I said.

'Oh really? What's your style?'

I thought about it. 'I guess you'd say I work from within a realist tradition.'

Jerome seemed to lose interest. This was not unusual. People tended to see portraits as fussy and conventional as opposed to abstract art. I sometimes thought the same, but I was too sincere. I just didn't have the disaffection modern art required.

'Why Vietnam?' Rick asked suddenly.

'There's a growing collector base here for local and international art,' I told them, as if that explained it. Then I recited some facts I'd learnt preparing for my application: that while social realism dominated up until the 1990s, by the early 2000s many artists had returned from Europe and America to start galleries and collectives. Some of that radical energy was still around.

'Are there many issues with censorship?' asked Scotty.

This I did not know. I had only a vague conception of Vietnamese politics, derived from films and high school textbooks. I knew a few of the big artists, like Dinh Q Lê, whose work with photographs had moved me deeply when I saw them, but in reality I had little idea who I was talking about, or what made up the scene I was referencing, or what indeed the censorship amounted to. I hesitated, but Rick had changed the subject anyway.

Talk moved on to Scotty's hair loss.

'It's the stress of all this shit with Carly,' he said pitifully, staring into his glass. I felt bad for him, but not enough. I insisted on buying everyone another round, and when I got back to our table, Jerome was telling everybody how he'd heard that guys who lost their hair had more testosterone.

'That's why women go crazy for bald guys,' he concluded. 'They can smell the pheromones or something. Look at that little English fucker, the one in those Transformer movies.'

'Jason Statham,' Martin volunteered.

'*Exactement*. And Vin Diesel, the big American. When he comes out, the girls go wild.'

Martin flushed. 'When you think about it, there are heaps!' He counted on his fingers. 'Bruce Willis, The Rock, Common, Billy Zane, fucking Seal.'

'JK Simmons,' said Scotty.

'JK Simmons...Scotty... What the fuck.'

'My mother used to like Yul Brynner, and she was very *collet monté*, you know, uptight,' said Jerome, as if this observation decided things. 'You see,

I already watched this docuseries about the sexual lives of primates. They say that in the wild, male apes with less testosterone develop bigger balls.' He cupped a pair of imaginary testes in his hands.

Rick was incredulous. 'What's it got to do with Scotty's fucking head?'

'Everything, *mon ami, tout*!' Jerome cried.

Martin giggled. Scotty, hearing himself compared at first to Statham and then an ape, beamed confusedly.

Rick scowled. 'You're perverse, Jez,' he said, going off to smoke.

I wished I had the wherewithal to meet some decent people.

MUM FACETIMED REGULARLY to check I was 'making the most of it'. When I was little she'd given up her PhD in art history to work in a bank, and while she supported my practice, I sensed she also feared that art, for me as it had for her, would amount to nothing more than sacrifice and disappointment.

She usually called me on her lunchbreak. Because of the time difference, this meant I'd speak with her just after getting up. One such morning, I was lying in bed scrolling and judging people I went to school with, eating cold bún chả I'd carried home the night before, when I discovered that Alex, with whom I had a complicated friendship, had been awarded a fellowship in Ho Chi Minh City. I was knifed with envy. Hers not only carried more prestige, but it also paid a better stipend.

Mastering myself, I commented on her photo: *Come and visit!* followed by the jet emoji. This condescension made me feel generous, which I liked.

Mum materialised, sitting cross-legged in a park. The Birrarung slid lazily behind her. The tide was going out, exposing mud for ducks and moorhens to investigate, and away across the river I could see the flashing windows of Crown Plaza and the crowds that amassed at Southbank over lunch. It provoked an unexpected pang of longing and I gagged a little on a noodle. Suddenly, I felt so lonely I was sick.

Mum was eating salad. 'What are you having?' she asked, chewing excitedly.

'Um...bún.'

'Ooh. What's that?'

'We've had it at that place in Footscray. It's, like, rice noodles and grilled pork.'

'Sounds good. I don't remember.'

'It's alright. It's cold.'

'Is it always cold?'

'No, I'm just eating it cold.'

'Why?'

'I got it last night.'

'What were you doing last night?'

'I went out. I dunno.'

'Alright! Why are you being cagey?'

'I'm not being cagey.'

'Right. Well, anyway, I was talking to Jane the other day,' she said, changing direction. 'Her daughter Siena said your new paintings are getting all this attention.'

'That's weird. Which ones?'

'The new ones. Jane said Siena said you're doing formalist blues. I said it didn't sound like you.'

This was strange. I tried to picture them. 'Where did Siena say she saw them?'

'They're all over the internet, apparently.'

'Alex got a fellowship in HMC,' was all I said.

'Well, she deserves it. I know it's not about the money, but you could make some real earnings with these.'

I assumed she'd confused some old paintings for new, perhaps the series of formalist pieces I did for final crits. There was nothing wrong with them per se, except I thought they lacked something essential – something I could describe only as heart.

'Siena says you should get in touch with her,' Mum continued. 'You know she manages that gallery in Toorak. If things keep going the way they are, she might find you some buyers.'

Ending the call, I felt unsettled. I no longer had an appetite for my bún chả.

IN MAY IT was my birthday, which Rick said we should celebrate. It'd got warmer, and the expats turned up wearing thongs and singlets. Rick bought me a Singapore Sling and pulled me into his armpit and I wondered whether, if push came to shove, I would go for alpha Rick, critical Jerome, sidekick Martin or divorcing, baldy Scott. Jerome kissed me on both cheeks and caught my lip. I hoped it wouldn't come to that.

From the bar we went to a club where Rick bought a huge bottle of vodka shaped like a machine gun; I swallowed when he squirted some into my mouth and suddenly felt wasted. The others went to piss, leaving me and Scotty alone. Everything smelt drunk. Scotty looked me in the eyes and moved a little closer. Pink and purple lights glanced off his baldness, which tonight was shining like a mirror ball. I blinked a few times. His mouth moved, but I couldn't hear him.

'I googled you!' he was shouting. 'Your paintings are so cool.'

'Thank you.' I was oddly pleased.

'I mean…fuck…' He did another shot, squeezing the barrel of the gun into his own mouth and kind of sucking on it. 'When you said you were an artist, I was wasn't expecting the real deal.'

He placed his hand on my knee, and I sensed the dim stirrings of attraction. Maybe there *was* something sexy about bald guys? Scotty was shouting in my ear about the paintings, how looking at them felt like staring into the abyss. His eyes were shining – he seemed genuinely moved. His touch felt beautiful and some huge and inarticulate emotion sprang into my throat. I thought I might start sobbing, the way some people did while getting professionally massaged. It had been a long time, I realised, since I'd had physical contact with another person.

I tried tuning in to what he was saying. That my paintings resonated with him in a massive way. That they spoke to the human condition. 'It's all just a big search for meaning. We have no idea what we are doing, why we're here,' his voice cracked. The music pounded in my ears. 'Everyone jokes about my hair,' said Scotty. 'I know it's just banter, but it hurts.'

He embraced me then, and I knew we would not have sex. Instead, I held him gently, almost paternally, like his spirit guide or dad. What he really wanted, I thought, was to be close to the great artist for a while.

'All we can do is tell our truth,' I said disingenuously.

'Correct,' he slurred. 'It's the only thing separating us from the apes.'

ALEX EMAILED TO say she was visiting Hanoi and asked if she could stay in my apartment. I hated the idea despite it being my suggestion. She would find me sitting on my floor, eating noodles, or wandering aimlessly around Dong Xuan, stumbling through the neon riot of consumer goods, at once overstimulated and mildly dissociative, or sitting on the sill cutting my toenails, letting the clippings fall onto the cats asleep on lower rooftops, or later in the evening drinking with the expats. Never painting, far from the perfect resident I'd been playing, if not an imperialist then almost certainly a traitor to my sex, a lapsed white feminist who spent her evenings getting shit-faced with a bunch of tone-deaf, climacteric white men.

I called my mum in panic. 'Alex is coming to stay.'

'Really? That'll be fun.'

'I guess so.'

'What?'

'I dunno… You know what she's like.'

'What's she like?' asked Rick when I repeated this. 'Is she hot?'

Martin snorted. Jerome rolled his eyes. 'Have a bit of fucking class.'

I told them she looked like an artist. She was always cutting her hair and wearing paint-stained work pants and Salomon XTs. She was actually Vietnamese – her grandparents immigrated to Kuala Lumpur and then to Melbourne with her mother in the '70s. Growing up, she went to one of the more expensive private schools. I didn't know where her family got their money, but the school had a pottery studio and a swimming pool. In uni, she decided she was queer and fell out with her parents. Around this time, she started making all these mega-abstract impressionist pieces after Helen Frankenthaler, but angrier and more to do with sex. She'd even done some solo exhibitions, when I had only been in groups. It's because she started ticking 'queer-POC' on her applications, she once told me. 'I've got no scruples about it. Why should I?'

'Well, why should she?' asked Jerome.

The lesser parts of me were envious.

Technically, we both knew Alex was the better painter. Yet there was something in her work that looked like mockery – or made me feel she was mocking something I really cared for.

'Will we get to meet her?' asked Martin.

'Oh,' I said vaguely. 'Maybe. We might have other plans.'

THE MORNING HER plane got in, I decided to actually do what I wanted Alex to think I was doing and headed for my studio. On the way, I took my usual route through the market, pausing in front of a stall that appeared to be selling dolls. The dolls were made of wax and dressed in tiny North Face jackets, but some of their limbs were missing, and other parts of them deformed, the little puffy jackets pinned back here and there to accommodate their missing parts. It was upsetting; I didn't know what it meant.

Outside, the day was sunny, and the city bustled with a merry air of industry. I felt a little better as I reached the studio, where I was greeted warmly by the gallerist, a woman in an elegant áo dài.

'My name is Diem,' she said. 'It's great to finally meet you. I'm sorry our hours haven't aligned; I assume you have been busy – you must be very pleased.'

'Yes,' I said, but I was confused.

'Where exactly is the exhibition?'

I stared at her blankly.

'Lab 25 Shimokitazawa,' she answered for me. 'That's in Tokyo, right? I see you've become a favourite with this big collector, Manzoni. Is that his name? It was a nice profile in *Dispatch*. That's good press.'

I was silent.

She smiled. 'You must be so, so pleased.'

Lost for words, I shifted oddly on my feet, which made Diem laugh, as though she understood me.

'It must take some getting used to,' she said knowingly, drifting towards her office. 'We should talk about the group exhibition. It looks like you will be our star.'

I retreated to my studio, my thoughts refusing to cohere. I'd been there only once before and now a thick layer of dust had gathered on the desk and sills. Sitting down, I opened my laptop and searched 'Manzoni', varying the spelling until eventually my search divulged a Tuscan art collector named Alberto Manoni, working out of Florence. On his Instagram, he'd posted a series of new acquisitions: big, blue formalist canvases attributed to me.

The paranoia kicked in earnestly. I zoomed in on the photos and saw not just an imitation of my signature but my signature itself. I looked up Lab 25 Shimokitazawa, the one Diem had mentioned; there was a landing page with news of my upcoming exhibition, but the details were sketchy and I couldn't find a physical address. Besides some catalogues of past shows in which some unknown artists featured, the gallery had no provenance, no physical footprint. Shimokitazawa, I discovered, was just the name of some trendy neighbourhood in Tokyo.

Frantically, I searched my name and found more images: my paintings hanging in a gallery, my painting pride of place in someone's home, a bidding war between Manoni and another art collector that had driven up the prices. I found the *Dispatch* edition Diem had mentioned, which included an old photo clearly taken from my Facebook, accompanied by an interview where the journalist was asking what my paintings were about.

MY WORK ISN'T ABOUT ANYTHING, fake me had seemingly replied.

I ONLY FIND ART BEAUTIFUL WHEN IT'S TALKED ABOUT IN THE SUBJUNCTIVE.

THE POSSIBILITY IT REPRESENTS INSPIRES ME MORE THAN THE REALITY.

So, I guess you could say that it's about possibility?

NOT POSSIBILITY – FAILURE.

ART'S FAILURE TO BE EVERYTHING WE LONG FOR IT TO BE.

I sounded esoteric and nonsensical. I sounded like an artist.

My chest constricted, and I realised it was not with terror but excitement. I was wretched with it: a feeling I was sure must be illegal. Strange, enthralling thoughts ran through my mind. A revenge plot by a person I had slighted. The work of some weird fan, a freak I went to school with. An elaborate scam by a bunch of fake collectors. An art-world hoax, a massive joke designed to force the market to confront its contradictions. There was something going on here, and it seemed to be about representation. I was its victim, but I was also its star. For some reason, I thought of the creepy dolls I had seen earlier, at the market. I sat there for a long time, considering my next move.

ALEX WAITED AT the door to my apartment. She appeared triumphant, and for a second I suspected her.

'How long have you been here?' I asked darkly.

'Just arrived. Why do you sound suspicious?' she joked, following me up the stairs.

After she'd showered, we went to my usual bar and found a table by the window. We ordered margaritas. The sun grew warmer. Sweat trickled down my back.

'This bar seems kind of middle-aged.'

'It's just convenient,' I justified. 'We're really near my studio.'

Alex was watching me fidget. 'What's up with you? You seem like you're on edge.'

'Something happened.'

'What?'

'Something massive.'

'Is this about the paintings? They're amazing. It's like they came out of thin air. Everyone is talking about you.'

'Alex, they're not –'

'Stop doing that. It's frustrating, you're gaslighting yourself. You know,' she said, licking the salt rim off her margarita, 'we chronically underestimate our value.'

I spread my hands, appealing. 'But it's all a big joke!' I cried. I felt like I was acting.

'And?' she shrugged. 'So is modern art.'

We were silent for a moment. 'Do you really think they're good?'

'I think they're brilliant,' Alex replied.

'You don't understand. I didn't do –'

'You did, and they're beautiful. Listen… If you spoke about other people the way you're talking now, they'd think you were a bitch. We're all so painfully self-critical. I'm sick of it. I'm trying to work on it, myself.'

I felt desperate and it thrilled me. 'I'm not saying I'm untalented…'

'Well, that's what I'm hearing.' Alex finished her drink. 'Want another one? I'll get it this time. I am fucking flush.'

Towards evening, the expats arrived. Alex mocked them all and I could see Jerome and Rick falling in love with her. She showed off her language skills, telling them that she was Viet Kieu – overseas Vietnamese – touching their arms, showing pictures of her art. Then she pulled up Instagram and showed them pictures of my paintings.

'Amazing,' said Martin. 'I can't believe you've been keeping all this talent under wraps.'

I looked around shiftily. It felt like one of those dreams where you're driving a car and the brakes fail. It was too late to do anything about it – the situation was already beyond my control.

While the expats got another round of drinks, Alex pulled me aside and demanded that we go somewhere more fun.

'There's no way we're taking those guys,' she said, grabbing my phone, asking for the passcode and then scrolling through my emails. 'Let's smoke-bomb.'

Suddenly, we were on the street and it was very hot and lively. Alex hailed a cab and gave the driver the address and then we were at a gallery, lining up. A tiny, fashionable person rushed over, introducing herself as Suong. Her head was shaved, and she looked nothing like I'd pictured.

'I can't believe you're here,' she said warmly. 'I've been emailing you a lot.'

I felt stupid as we followed her around. The walls were hung with giant, wall-sized prints depicting market stalls selling many incongruous things. One of them was familiar, and I stopped, only realising after I had stared at it for ages that it showed the very stall I'd paused outside this morning, the one that sold those strange, unnerving dolls. Together, we surveyed their missing limbs.

'Agent Orange,' Suong explained. 'It's a radical critique. The jackets represent consumerism. The hypocrisy of the West.'

I stood there guiltily. 'Yeah,' I said.

We walked around. Suong was friends with everyone, and some other residents came and introduced themselves. When they asked me what I did, Alex got out her phone.

'She's going to be famous. Have a look at this.'

Immediately, a cold sweat bloomed all over me. It was one thing to fool the expats, but now I tried to snatch the phone. 'Please!' I said intensely. 'Don't!'

Suong frowned, looking up from the screen. 'But they're so good,' she said simply. 'What are you afraid of?'

Back at my apartment, Alex said again how much she liked the paintings.

'They're so…I don't know, exciting. Don't take this the wrong way, but I'm glad you've got away from all that realist shit. I get that it's meant to represent the struggle or whatever, but to be honest I always wondered what exactly you were trying to say. It's not like here, where if you're doing something new there's still a risk you'll be censored. We're privileged in Australia. Art doesn't have to mean anything. We can paint whatever we want.'

I stared up at the ceiling, listening to her voice reach through the darkness.

'What were you even doing before I got here? You weren't just hanging with those expats…'

'Hardly ever,' I said, another massive lie.

ALEX STAYED FOR one week, and in that time my residency changed completely. It was summer and Hanoi was fat with storms and heat and vigour. We went everywhere, did everything. Without quite knowing how it happened, I was living the life I'd been faking for my friends and family back home.

Our friendship with Suong was fast and there were places she would take us: workshops and parties and committees and openings, and the humidity soared and the noonday sun burst quickly into heavy bouts of rain; the streets were full and tourists lingered round the little temples, buying souvenirs and fruit cups from the vendors plying trade.

Suong shared an apartment with a guy called Van, who introduced us to the city's pop-punk scene; we went to gigs where tiny singers shouted words I couldn't understand, although I felt their protest rise within and raised my fist with all the rest. We caught up with some Danish friends of Alex's who were passing through, and I had sex with one of them – he wasn't bald. The expats texted, but I didn't answer.

Just before her flight back down to HMC, we walked around the lake. Hordes of people milled about, and we linked arms, looking at the lights on the water.

'I'm glad I came,' said Alex.

'Me too.'

She grinned. 'But I'm looking forward to getting back into the studio after slacking off all week.'

My pulse sped up. 'Yeah. Totally.'

'You're going to have to work like hell to finish everything for the exhibition.'

She was looking off into the distance and I watched her slyly, fighting a mad impulse of sincerity. But the feeling dissipated just as soon as it arrived. Instead, I agreed with her. 'Yes,' I said, simply. 'I know.'

After she left, I walked slowly to my studio. Alex was right. I needed to get to work.

IN THE FINAL weeks of my residency, I made up for lost time. My studio became a mess of drop sheets and the remnants of my meals. I wore paint-stained work pants and some fake Salomon XTs I'd got at Hang Da. I liked the early mornings best, when the humidity was still low and I could drink a strong iced coffee before starting on my copies.

My training had equipped me with the necessary technique, and freed from the burden of my earnestness, I started painting better than I'd ever painted in my life. I filled those massive canvases with blue, and it didn't take long for it to feel completely natural, like something I had always done.

Before leaving Hanoi, I applied for funding on the strength of my renown. Rumours had begun to circulate. A journalist emailed, claiming to know Alberto Manoni was a fake collector and the whole thing was a hoax. She asked if I was aware that I'd been used as a pawn in his demented machinations. I wrote back cryptically. 'Have you ever been influenced by something you've never seen? Do you have to physically view an artwork to believe in its existence?'

Meanwhile, my DMs filled with enquiries and invitations to exhibit work. Inspired by my interaction with the journalist, I claimed the whole thing as my project, suggesting that the rumours raised questions about the legitimisation of art and artists in the age of social media. I implied that maybe it was all a clever demonstration of how easy it's becoming to manipulate the market. 'The story makes the art more interesting,' I wrote as I applied for funding. 'The myths surrounding its creation have become part of the work.'

The day I was to leave Hanoi, I gave my North Face jacket to a man outside my building. It was no longer raining, but my fingers clattered on the keyboard. 'Who is the artist concealed behind the signature?' I typed. 'Who gets to decide what's fake?'

Almost fondly, I remembered the expats. 'I paint my own reality,' I wrote, getting on a roll. *You like that, Rick?* I thought – *that's me quoting Frida Kahlo.* I hoped they would be awed, even touched, by the time they'd spent with me. I was still addressing them as I caught a taxi to the airport, checked my bags and cleared security. *You want some of this, Jerome? You like that, Martin? How about you, Scotty?* I monologued. *I'm the real fucking deal.*

Miriam Webster's first book, a collection of short stories called *The Slip*, was published in 2025 with Aniko Press. She lives in Naarm/Melbourne, where she is working on a novel as part of a PhD in Creative Writing at the University of Melbourne. Her fiction, essays and poetry have appeared in exhibitions, major prizes, journals, books, online and on the sides of buildings, including in publications like *Aniko Magazine, HEAT, Island, Overland, The Suburban Review, swim meet lit mag* and certain zines.

Anders Villani

Libretti

You spend your Centrelink payment on a dinner package to the opera. *Madama Butterfly*. You rent a suit, tie, waistcoat, black, black, black, starched white shirt. A man with black hair and white regrowth takes your measurements. He blushes when you ask him to show you how to tie a tie and he has no idea, he hasn't had this job long, not that you'd have known, not that he knows what you've done. *Di rincorrerla furor m'assale, se pure infrangerne dovessi l'ale*. No shoe rentals. You buy a pair, $79.95 on Afterpay. Black loafers, silver *fleur-de-lis* buckles. You leave in character. You're a tenor. From the bag with the clothes and shoes you wore here you smell vanilla vape, drug sweat, coin metal – the funk of a fresh corpse. Your soles slide on the buffed shopping-centre floor like air-hockey pucks. See him, drinking a Coke spider from a clamshell milkshake glass no store here uses? Does he look familiar? Tell him you're off to the opera. I can't give you what you're asking for at the station, I'm off to the opera. *Madama Butterfly*. You head downtown, park at the peak of a multistorey. Hot wind soothes from somewhere. *Affonda l'ancora alla ventura*. Your suit's rumpled. Your dinner could be worse. It's French. It needs salt, but you're afraid you'll hurt the waiter. You tip lavishly. For most of the show a mist of incomprehension and perfume drapes, enchants you. You lead the ovation. Near the Shrine, you wade into a pond and become an eel. *Si, tutto in un istante io vedo il fallio mio*. Your mother calls. Your cousin played Pinkerton at La Scala. Renato Cioni. You google him. There he is, how dramatic, CCTV, your eyes, your suit, attacking a stranger as rush-hour carriages disgorge.

Anders Villani is the author of two poetry collections: *Aril Wire* (Five Islands Press, 2018) and *Totality* (Recent Work Press, 2022).

NON-FICTION

The tale of the innocents

Lactation, criminality and the economics of care

Lauren Carroll Harris

I WAS DUE to pick up my daughter, Orly, nine months old and all melting cheeks, from my friend Lily's place. I felt I was used to having a baby and ready to experiment with new ways to jigsaw mothering work (which doesn't pay) and writing (which pays a little). Lily, an absolute darling, had offered to take Orly for a couple of hours to play with her own daughter while I bunkered down in the library. I found Orly bright and relaxed upon my return.

'I tried to breastfeed her,' said Lily, who produced a proud and magnificent flow and had once described nursing as a 'joy'. 'But she just kind of looked up at me weirdly and pulled back and peered at my nipple.' It was such an unexpected yet kind, instinctive gesture on Lily's part – and so sensible.

'It seems unintuitive that she would refuse milk,' I frowned. 'I wonder if breastfeeding from someone other than me just kind of felt foreign to her. Smelt foreign, even.' I guessed Orly was a geriatric baby now, too accustomed to my hold and care alone.

I had, in this practical, uninvited way, a sense that breastfeeding could be a task shared beyond biological families. Lactation was becoming, for me, a great way to think about collectivity. Yet I found in conversations that the first association people made was the phenomenon of wet nursing: the most privatised manner in which lactation has historically been shared across biological boundaries. When we talk of breastfeeding today, we tend to speak about the burden of motherly labour – its isolation, its difficulty, its association with maternal shame and performance, pressure and perfection. Has it always been this way? A glance through the history books could help me, I thought. I had to be creative in my research methods: any action that isn't paid for generally exists in a miasma of historical murmur. But every now and then, a toiling scholar will uncover something new in the archives of care work that breaks every cultural assumption linking maternity, softness, nurturing and domesticity.

FROM THE 1400s to the 1800s, most towns of a certain size in France, Spain, Portugal and Italy had foundling hospitals, where poor or single mothers would deposit the babies for whom they could no longer care. The problem of abandoned babies (sometimes called 'throwaways') was also religious: Western Europe was facing an epidemic of unbaptised little souls. The foundling system was miserable for both children and adults. Many of the infants were born syphilitic and continued to communicate the disease to their wet nurses (wet nursing being a common practice across Catholic Europe in the Middle Ages and early modern period). Many of these babies couldn't be saved from the malnutrition and ill health they were born into; mortality rates were astonishingly high.

American historian Dr Erin Maglaque, who works at Sheffield University, has found sources pointing to the stories of hundreds of otherwise unattested women paid as wet nurses at one of the earliest such foundling hospitals, run by the Catholic Church in the Tuscan hills of Florence from 1445 onwards. The papers of the Church administration reveal something unusual: some of the wet nurses were declared to be defrauding the institution. Previous research had suspected 'fraudulent' wet nurses to be guilty of smothering, infanticide and run-of-the-mill child neglect. But Dr Maglaque told me over Zoom about a different 'scam':

> The wet nurses, especially in Florence, which is where most of my archival research has been, they're from the countryside, they take their infant to the foundling hospital in Florence, abandon the infant there. And then when the infant is reassigned to another wet nurse in the countryside, they track it down and swap the baby so they're being paid to breastfeed their own child. Which I just thought was

> absolutely wild. [Wet nursing] was pretty exploitative, they weren't paid that much. But if they had a recent birth or a child who died, then it was a good way to make an extra wage on top of what they were doing.

This grimly brilliant baby-moving scheme was an ingenious way for women to be paid by the Church to care for and stay close to their own children. In a neat coincidence, the women worked for the Spedale degli Innocenti, the Hospital of the Innocents: a refuge for orphans that built idealised and splendid images of angelic children into its architecture; the triangular stretches between arches still blaze with swaddled bambini in a gorgeous blue glazed terracotta.

'The women were paid a certain wage per month,' says Dr Maglaque. 'There was a flat rate if the baby was getting milk and then a flat rate once it was weaned. With wet nursing, you think it's only breastfeeding, but they were being paid to mother or parent the children. Really like a mother because it was a twenty-four-hour job.'

The term 'foster parent' might better reflect our contemporary understanding – except that theirs was an institutional life. The children were institutionalised too, eventually working as farm labourers. They were taught trades and apprenticeships, then brought back to the city to work in proto-industrial factories to make silk, lace and other textiles in a gloomy precursor to the child-staffed workhouses of Europe's future. Some girls earnt a dowry working for the Church, while a few entered the nunnery.

'The foundling hospitals themselves and the friars – the men who ran them – referred to themselves as the father[s] of the children,' Dr Maglaque tells me. 'The babies were called the sons and daughters of the house. They had a strong institutional identity.'

'I study the material reality among these poor people,' she continues. 'Their attitude was that milk is a finite resource. It was treated by the authorities as if it wasn't, but it was.' This reality was far from the private world of bourgeois wet nursing but rather a kind of large-scale, waged version overseen by Church values.

All women's domestic labour is finite and takes a heavy bodily toll. Breastfeeding requires calories, sleep and rest; fatigue and illness can set in, lives can end, and there are only so many hours in a day. The difference now is that such reproductive work is assumed and silenced in a different institution: the atomised single-family home. 'Under capitalism,' Dr Maglaque explains, 'it's always the natural environment and women's labour that are both positioned as a resource that will never run out, and obviously that's not true and the harm is then distributed to the women at the bottom. And the children. That's the other part of it. Sometimes children or infants are left out of how we think about that exploitation. And that's just not something we ever really talk about.'

Dr Maglaque's translated sources are disturbingly to the point: entry and exit registers recording the admission of an infant, naming them and the date of their subsequent death. Tapping a button on her Zoom screen, she shows me a spectral picture of one of the cases she's been looking at, a dusty little scrap from another world:

> This one is Agnolino, that's the name of the baby. January 1570 – when he was left at the hospital. He was just barely wrapped in *cativo*, so a piece of wool, or like a poor piece of linen or swaddling. And then it says when he was given to the wet nurses and how much they were paid. The last record here is a little happier. That baby's name is Bacio, and he's with a wet nurse named Lucia. And it says he was visited on the 4th of May 1604.

Sta benne, the record states laconically: *was well.*

THE RECORDS HARDLY reflect the never-ending nature of wet-nursing work. The rural Innocenti women were also sharecroppers, tenant farmers who paid their rent as portions of their harvest, punctuating their child-bearing years with wet-nursing wages to top up their farm work. They toted their foundling charges around with them while they distributed feed to animals, collected eggs, cooked, cleaned, made cheese, gathered wood, tended fire, spun and wove textiles, gardened, harvested, soaped and hung laundry, hauled produce to markets and sold their goods. The invention of powdered baby formula was centuries away, and though there were other creative, imperfect feeding methods (from other mammals' milk dripped from a perforated cow's horn to slurries of bread, sugar and water), the nurses' milk was therefore essential to babies' survival. For their monthly wage, the women probably fed their foundling Church babies on demand – as well as swaddling, watching and carrying them day and night. A census-keeper today would classify this work as farming, trading and parenting, and it earnt less than the work of a gardener or shopkeeper. The wage decreased upon weaning, but children remained in the wet nurse's care.

Being a wet nurse also meant being subject to a network of surveillance under the gaze of the *riveditore*, or overseer: Church men who would visit, monitor the children's growth and gather intelligence on a wet nurse's performance. The terms were strict and amounted to no less than a total loss of bodily autonomy. To continue earning her wage, the wet nurse had to be audited and deemed clean enough, good enough and completely chaste. That the spring and summer harvests marked the times when a child was most likely to be abandoned to the Church is testimony to the aggrieved, taxing nature of combined farming, breastfeeding and caregiving.

'If they detected fraud, they took the baby away from the mother, and in almost every case that I found, the baby died,' says Dr Maglaque. Discovering the fraud, however, was difficult and required a denouncement from a local informant to a *riveditore* – until a new strategy of brutality was enacted: 'In the second half of the seventeenth century, some foundling hospitals in Italy started branding or tattooing the feet of the babies to keep track of them... So, the hospital administrator could look immediately and know, and that would stop a certain amount of fraud.'

The Church thought it was milking (pun absolutely intended) the poor women; indeed, it couldn't find enough of them to employ – until in 1770 it finally stopped its policy of farming out hungry babies to peasant women before closing the rotating window in 1875 that allowed parents to anonymously deposit their babies. The mythology of the Innocenti foundling hospital continues to warp online, with strange, unverifiable claims that Mussolini lived there as a child in the late nineteenth century. Some historians estimate that the Innocenti took in a total of 375,000 castaway children over the centuries. I think of the desperate, defrauding, criminal wet nurses as creating their own early form of parenting payment – or a perverse, pre-modern baby bonus – long before the advent of the welfare state, back when the European landscape was flecked with spires rather than civic town halls. For their reproductive labour, the women found a way to extract a dirty payment with which to raise their own children on the Church's dime – a hidden history of women's worth.

FOR DR MAGLAQUE, these tricky wet nurses were, in their own manner, centuries-long precursors to Silvia Federici, the Marxist feminist who wrote in 1975 that women should receive wages for housework. Born in Italy, Federici moved to the US to pursue a PhD and established a Wages for Housework office in Brooklyn, distributing literature, participating in activism and arguing that we are all the product of invisible, unvalued housework. Like other 1970s feminists, Federici imagined that every glistening countertop, grimy dinner plate, dash to the shops and midnight breastfeed should be recognised as a form of employment – and asserted that this kind of essential labour never really ended, just as the Florentine wet nurses had experienced centuries earlier. Across the echoes of time, the logic is shared: that the home is a workplace, and that caregiving is productive labour and essential to the continuation of society itself; it should therefore be remunerated the same way as waged labour.

'One of the achievements of the International Wages for Housework Campaign…was precisely to unmask not only the amount of work that unwaged houseworkers do for capital but, with that, the social power that this work potentially confers on them, as domestic work reproduces the worker and consequently it is the pillar of every other form of work,' said Federici in 2013, still ever the hardcore Marxist. 'We saw an example of this power – the power of refusal – in October 1975, when women in Iceland went on strike and everything in Reykjavik and other parts of the country where the strike took place came to a halt.' I love that Federici never changed her position. Nor did she ever marry her partner. In her view, housework is naturalised by the institution of marriage.

The divergence between Federici and the Florentine wet nurses lies in the fact that the latter were involved in a social contract conferred by their payment from the Catholic Church. They were formally recognised as workers in a struggle, a perverse demonstration of Federici's theory. Sometimes the Florentine mothers tried to negotiate more pay; Dr Maglaque has found documentation of these fluctuating figures in the archives. The contentious issue was one of motherly kinship: if the wet nurses were related to their children, they were deemed undeserving of pay. In that case, the

Church's judgement was that they were just mothering – almost a slur – which should be fulfilling enough. But if the women were nursing children not biologically theirs, their provision of lifegiving milk and care was seen as legitimate work. This is the hard line that still determines whose labour is valued in the home. It's only unusual to see it declared so unilaterally in monetary terms.

In this sense, the Spedale degli Innocenti system for wet nursing is flagrant about the values that we still find difficult to denaturalise today. We live so deep inside the institutions of the family, gender and motherhood that it can be hard to defamiliarise ourselves with the fact of their constructedness. Biological reproduction is the mechanism that can be exploited in order to make women the unpaid nurturers of the next generation of labourers and citizens – as long as you can convince mothers that they're carrying out love's labour. Beyond that, the wet nurses were engaged in a form of organised resistance to patriarchal rule, activating whisper networks of communication to arrange contact with their children and hear of the approaching *riveditore*. This was not moral deviance; it was honest, shining resistance.

The Florentine women couldn't have known that they anticipated, by almost five hundred years, the feminist push in the 1970s to include unpaid labour in economic outputs. These calls had been raised by the late nineteenth century in the West: by Charlotte Perkins Gilman in the US and independent politician Eleanor Rathbone in the UK (though the latter's campaign resulted in welfare, not wages). Yet economists are still grappling with how to account for the contribution of care to society: I heard a highly respected political scientist recently state with absolute authority that the family exists in a realm separate to the economy, which is where the market, value, money and labour reside. One feminist economist I have spoken to believes that breastfeeding should be included in the Gross Domestic Product (GDP), just as sex work and illegal drug sales are included in Europe's accounting systems, and that exclusion from the GDP is a feminine freebie to capitalism.

It's common, too, to see social media posts by radicalising mothers declaring that many women spend an estimated 1,800 hours breastfeeding, roughly equivalent to a full-time job, in the first year of their child's life. Grappling with time seems to be a better form of quantification than monetary worth – except that it implies women can't work or do anything else *except* breastfeed, which is yet another powerful cultural myth.

Breastfeeding exists on a timeline of biological reproduction, a through-line of ovulation, conception, gestation, birth and then lactation. But the provision of breastmilk can be understood through another framework that's not strictly maternal. Human milk exists on the same spectrum of biological materials as blood and organs. It can perch awkwardly in a gift economy: one in which my friend Lily's effort to breastfeed Orly might have taken place, had Orly not refused – the kind of 'baseline communism' referred to by anarchist anthropologist David Graeber.

Or it can exist in a world of shadow pricing – that is, the pricing allocated when there's no market value for your activity, and so the value of a similar activity is used in its place. In 1995, the Fourth World Conference on Women pushed for changes in the rules for the national accounting systems to allow the counting of subsistence agriculture, much of which is engaged in by women. This push created a precedent for mother's milk to be counted. Most breastmilk is not bought and sold, but it *could* be – and could therefore attain a shadow price.

'Women contribute to development not only through remunerated work but also through a great deal of unremunerated work,' said the Beijing Platform and Declaration for Action, adopted in 1995:

> On the one hand, women participate in the production of goods and services for the market and household consumption, in agriculture, food production or family enterprises. Though in the United Nations System of National Accounts and therefore in international standards for labour statistics, this 'unremunerated work – particularly that related to agriculture – is often undervalued and under-recorded. On the other hand, women still also perform the great majority of unremunerated domestic work and community work. This work is often not measured in quantitative terms and is not valued in national accounts. The full visibility of the type, extent and distribution of this unremunerated work will also contribute to a better sharing of responsibilities.

This platform for action was subsequently endorsed by the United Nations General Assembly.

Some scholars say that GDP is itself a myth that the economy will always far exceed, especially at a time when automation is displacing more service provision into consumers' own hands – for example, when I order a salad at a café via a QR code or scan my own groceries at a supermarket. It seems that nobody can agree, in either practice or theory, on what should be remunerated, let alone how to place a value on caring for children, sick and the aged, on family food preparation, on protecting the environment and on providing voluntary assistance to vulnerable and disadvantaged individuals and groups. These are the very places where women's contributions to economic development are not counted – and are therefore not socially recognised.

The notion of GDP wasn't formalised until 1934, but Dr Maglaque's findings strike me as especially disruptive to the idea that only activities with a market value have economic worth: some types of care work were commercialised half a millennium ago in an agricultural Christian society; the assumption that care between kin should be unpaid predates our modern era, too. 'In the face of this commercialisation,' wrote Dr Maglaque in a peer-reviewed paper from 2022, 'the ideological edifice of infant care as a "natural" facet of motherhood looks more fragile.'

Ultimately, I sense that her research is more interested in the wet nurses' resistance to their exploitation than the potentially impossible measurement of that exploitation. Defining the line between waged and unwaged work as kinship and biological relation was essential to the lie being sold by the Church. We bring the same logic today to the cleaners and childcare workers who are differentiated from 'voluntary' mothers: we value paid labour with an employer over unpaid work. Once a woman chooses motherhood, she's deemed complicit in this logic.

That women used wet-nursing wages to create an illicit social support system challenges any natural notion of maternal bonds, particularly those in patriarchal societies. The Innocenti's wet nurses occupied a singular moment in time: early modernity and the rise of capitalism, which would subsume sharecropping and other essentially feudal forms of work. We might bring other labour perspectives to the women's battle. The wet nurses weren't incorporated into a guild or organisation, their time wasn't organised into discrete blocks of work and leisure, and they had few rights (indeed, they lived in a time before the contingent idea of universal human rights). They bore the double burden of caregiving as well as farming tasks. They were fortunate to survive child-bearing, but they were depleted by their lifetime cycle of pregnancy, birth and lactation. Syphilis was their occupational hazard. They had to work together to reconnect to their once renounced babies and hide their kinship from the *riveditore*. But their work had statistical representation in the Church's accounting system.

The evolving class structure and industrial time regime that made wet nursing and sharecropping redundant never addressed care work. Now, more than ever, when the cost for caregiving is imposed on individuals within ever smaller nuclear family units, an abundance of cultural stories normalises this exploitation: motherhood manuals like *What to Expect When You're Expecting*, Hollywood pregnancy comedies, the religious iconography of the Madonna breastfeeding the baby Jesus in holy passivity, the 'fertility and pregnancy' pages of cursed women's media like *Mamamia*, the images of feminine optimisation generated by every mumfluencer on Instagram and TikTok (not to mention the much-debated pregnant bellies of tradwives). Even progressive cultural discussions of family-making accept the exploitative logic of mothers' lives.

When Miranda July, known for her disruptive radicalism, posted to her Substack a deleted passage from her recent novel, *All Fours* (2024), vacillating on whether to have children, she did just that: 'If we described the hardship of a mother's life accurately, in practical terms ("unless you have money you won't have very much time for your creative work, yourself, or even your children") we might actually cause a woman to change her mind, and this feels like playing God.' Would challenging the terms of kinship like the Florentine wet nurses be like playing God, too, or can we not imagine a better community structure for giving and receiving care than the family?

MY DAUGHTER, ORLY, will most likely be my greatest contribution to the economy in naked GDP terms. If I follow the logic Dr Maglaque has established, I have to ask why I was issued a poverty-line payment for six months of parental leave but not for the time that follows. I could not share the parental leave with other beloved significant others, which reinforces the logic of biological, primary caregiving. (I love to imagine having shared my parental leave with a close friend or extended family member, and the potential effect in enlarging the family unit and sphere of love and care around Orly.) If I have another child, I will receive superannuation as part of my parental leave, a mechanism that did not exist when my first child was born – yet another arbitrary incongruity.

This fraught history of family, labour and payment, be it through wages or welfare, is far from resolved; it's reflected in almost all the cultural narratives we tell about the hardships of motherhood. Virulent strains of liberal feminism continue to champion paid work at the expense of unpaid work. Likewise, breastfeeding remains a huge source of anxiety and trouble for mothers today – under-supported, stricken sometimes with social stigma, marketed against by formula companies, posited as a choice rather than a right and a public health issue, and made difficult by workplaces and precarious work.

I have entered motherhood at a different time, but I can sense the women's vexation in the archival notations of the *riveditore*: 'Baby Domenico is well, but doesn't stand up any more, and the wet-nurse doesn't want to keep him unless something more is given to her.' I don't think the wet nurse was talking just about the money, and nor was Silvia Federici. There remains a huge sham, a black hole, at the centre of society's idea of what drives it, challenged theoretically but not resolved by the imaginative politics of Wages for Housework.

I like to think that what truly binds the Innocenti's hidden system and Wages for Housework is the notion that caregiving and activism are the secret engines of society and change. I saw Federici's blistering critiques rise up again during the pandemic, when the phrase 'essential labour' unveiled the naturalisation of care in households, which were then locked down and churning in a 24/7 family economy of homeschooling, salaried work and domestic labour. Quite suddenly, the *New York Times* was profiling an elderly Federici, who was newly consumed by caring for her ageing partner – a form of labour she also described as 'reproduction'. I then saw interest in Wages for Housework wane again as we seemed to adjust to the new norms of post-pandemic life, forgetting about those early, incendiary calls to reshape the world in a more equal manner. Then, eventually, the Innocenti wet nurses floated across Google Scholar towards me.

The downfall of the archives relayed by Dr Maglaque through my Zoom window is, almost predictably, the absence of the words and perspectives of the women themselves toiling in the hills of Florence, Siena and San Gimignano. They will always be mediated, faceless. I love these women, whoever they were. Theirs are the deep stories that show us how shadow systems of value are where life truly ticks on. These are the stories on which the world has spun, and continues to spin, even if the names and lives of the women themselves remain obscured by the monetary focus of the Church archives. Capitalism still runs the most incredible shakedown on caregivers. But some submerged knowledge will always return to the surface, somehow.

Lauren Carroll Harris' cultural criticism has appeared in *Sydney Review of Books*, *Brooklyn Rail*, *Los Angeles Review of Books*, *Lit Hub*, Radio National, ABC TV, *Open Secrets: Essays on the Writing Life* (Giramondo Publishing, 2022) and *Outside the Frame: Art and the Moving Image* (Perimeter Books, 2024). A former casual academic, she has a PhD in cinema from UNSW. Her debut non-fiction book, *We Don't Belong to Ourselves*, will be published by Ultimo Press in 2027.

NON-FICTION

The cost of living

Hidden histories of the Defence Site Maribyrnong

Timmah Ball

The key is to read along and against the archive grain, to shed light on these records, interrogate their origins, and activate some awakening to reckon with it all.

– Natalie Harkin, 2025

THE ONLY TIME the public was allowed to enter the explosives factory was on family day. The one-off event occurred in December 1960 to celebrate the factory's fiftieth year in operation. Curious onlookers watched factory workers manufacture military weapons, bullets, cordite power and other ammunition: hazardous jobs equivalent to handling radioactive material in a nuclear power plant, requiring extreme precaution. But family day allowed friends and relatives to understand the complex and dangerous work their loved ones pursued, an opportunity that feels slightly macabre but is not dissimilar to the many contemporary tourist experiences offered at former prisons, concentration camps and massacre sites.

I came across the disused factory along the Maribyrnong River during the Covid pandemic and found myself absorbed by the array of dormant buildings, abandoned and fenced off behind barbed wire. It was strange to imagine that this vacant site, nestled among shrubs and bushland, had once been the largest weapons manufacturer on the continent, established in 1910 as the Maribyrnong Explosives Factory and owned by the Australian Department of Defence. Among the overgrown grass and decaying buildings were smaller cottages and huts that lured me towards something, as if I could almost see a figure, a human presence within the empty terrain. I tried to imagine future possibilities that could revive the site. But its history, both peculiar and bleak, was more compelling to speculate on.

Having stood behind the domineering fence and read the Commonwealth signs prohibiting entry, I realised the quickest point of access was online. Quick Google searches turned into trails of disparate threads and dead ends in the archives as I tried to understand the presence I felt, the events that might have happened there and why such a large site, close to the city, bounded by the river and parklands, was being left to decay. I moved through council strategies, historical recordings and heritage plans with an urgency that felt like a betrayal of the delicate care Narungga poet and academic Natalie Harkin demands in her archival research. I couldn't ease my desire to know more about this ominous site: a place I couldn't enter but that was obsessively occupying my thoughts.

SITUATED ON HORSESHOE Bend, a unique curve in the river's topography, the Maribyrnong Explosives Factory became operational in 1912, employing fifty-three staff. Historian Les McLean describes residents observing that the 'scenic beauty was rather spoiled' by this establishment, which would grow exponentially thanks to the munitions demands of two world wars. By 1936, a chemical section had been built where more than two hundred different products were manufactured, the main one being TNT for bombs.

At this point, the factory was solely staffed by men, but as the Second World War unfolded, much of this demographic was enlisted, so women started working there too. Any gender biases regarding their capabilities soon diminished: most of these women were employed in physical roles, filling shells, bombs and detonators with TNT. Weaponry requirements increased when Japan entered the war, and 8,391 people were working at the site by 1942, at least half of them women.

Most of these people had no prior experience of working with explosives. It's difficult to fathom how it must have felt to handle toxic material as an unskilled worker pulled in to meet demand. McLean notes the policy and procedure guidelines in place at the time, which claim that the 'comparatively low fire and explosion records during the period of high production, coupled with extreme dilution of skilled labour, may be largely ascribed to the efficient "day to day" policing of rules and regulations'.

But these rules and regulations obscure the risk these workers were exposed to and pacify the volatile explosive products they were paid to make. The noise of machinery making bombs and bullets during this era is a jarring contrast to the eerie silence that now pervades the abandoned area – a silence that has carried through into my research. The historical accounts I've found frequently reference the lack of skilled labour, a detail that seems to fortify the factory's success: even with an inexperienced workforce, it delivered. These accounts never give the slightest hint that injuries or accidents occurred, which seems odd given the inherent danger of the work.

If its former role as a weapons manufacturer contributed to global cycles of war and violence – cycles that feel almost inescapable – its long-term vacancy alludes to several other misfortunes of colonial capitalism. The 127.8-hectare site, while still owned by the Department of Defence, ceased operations in 1994, when it could no longer safely produce high explosives within the abutting residential surrounds. Maribyrnong City Council started exploring options for the site in the late 1990s, offering a vision of affordable and social housing, local job growth, and leisure and recreational opportunities, all the while preserving the natural environment and celebrating the site's heritage and history.

But in the thirty-one years since its closure, the site has remained inert, despite a succession of master plans, urban design frameworks and private sector interest – plans that have started and stopped abruptly, reflecting the tenuous nature of planning under governments whose economic imperatives continue to supersede anything else.

In 2018, the Victorian Planning Authority (VPA) published the *Defence Site Maribyrnong Statement of Policy Intent*. Its objective was to 'establish capacity for a resident population of around 6,900 people, 3,300 dwellings and 1,800 jobs'. That same year, the VPA held detailed community consultation workshops to affirm their vision and gather local aspirations, work that seemed to repeat previous community engagement sessions led by VicUrban (now Development Victoria) in 2010. Participants across both engagements resoundingly desired affordable housing options that maintained the environmental values of the Maribyrnong River while improving transport linkages and other opportunities, such as jobs and recreational facilities, goals that feel necessary for any government to achieve on vacant land in a city where – like many others – homelessness, inequality, housing unaffordability and a plethora of interdependencies are growing. But the possibility of change remains as stagnant as the land left to decline.

To suggest that redeveloping the 127.8-hectare site is straightforward erases the layers of bureaucracy and economic decision-making at play. Much smaller sites in expensive neighbourhoods, such as the former Fitzroy Gasworks park, have taken decades to be developed, which illustrates that even when return on investment is strong, major civic and housing projects are still time-consuming and complex to deliver. But however difficult infrastructure delivery might be, the prolonged indecision that often surrounds them reflects a political and planning ethos of apathy, an unwillingness to imagine something better, something that would drive the change required to respond to the challenging dynamics of contemporary cities. Instead, sites like Maribyrnong fester in uncertainty, unable to justify the intergenerational benefits that would outweigh the financial cost of development. A cost inextricably linked to the site's past.

WHEN I FIRST looked through the barbed-wire fence, the site's dense greenery seemed to indicate a thriving environment where native plant species survive among the introduced weeds and dormant buildings. But after sifting through each of the studies, frameworks, plans, historical documents and community engagement reports I could find, I realised this surface vitality masks damaged soil: a consequence of all the bullets and shells produced here, which also contributed to sickness among staff. The unnerving scale of this damage was revealed when I learnt that the small curves in the landscape, which look like hills, almost, from certain vantage points, are actually earth-mound blast walls that were erected to test bombs and other explosives during the factory's operation. The land is rotten, with weaponry, chemicals and explosive waste oozing into the dirt as if its former industrial use has continued, interrupting the chance for something else to ever occur.

The cost to remediate the hazardous substances littered through the soil is estimated at $200 million – an expensive outlay, but the only way to rehabilitate the area and allow people to live there safely. This figure seems prohibitively large, coupled with the substantial resources needed to plan and build. But to do nothing is even worse. Leaving the site in its current state means that another heaviness looms, as if there's something else buried much deeper: histories, people and events that are far more difficult to reconcile than the pollutants requiring removal.

In 1998, a heritage study and assessment of the site was carried out by the consultancy firm Allom Lovell & Associates on behalf of Maribyrnong City Council. In the final report, it seems obvious from the introduction that certain limitations were imposed on the environmental and heritage surveys. Midway through, the authors acknowledge that the bulk of findings were conducted through desktop research and analysis. The only section of the site they physically inspected was the Engineering Development Establishment building, which didn't open until 1997 – meaning that the significant contamination generated by the factory's peak production during both wars wasn't accurately quantified. Access to all other areas was prohibited, with the study concluding that further assessment was required to thoroughly understand the extent of damage.

In 1999, a separate study was commissioned by Maribyrnong City Council to manage and protect the Aboriginal cultural heritage of the area. Similarly, this study noted that obtaining access permission was delayed, and visits were constrained by the intrinsic danger of the area. Because the site hadn't been cleared of unexploded ordinance, the consultants were required to remain on property access roads at all times and could move off the roads only if accompanied by a Defence representative. All the consultants involved in the inspection also had to remain together as a group for safety reasons, which limited the amount of time available to inspect specific areas.

In light of these factors, it becomes easier to speculate why it's so difficult to access the site, where bombs and grenades are still embedded, potentially left to explode by anyone compelled to go beyond the barbed-wire fence. This reckless and unnerving possibility evokes the unfathomable destruction that these weapons helped create. Maybe it's an area and era better left untouched, the stories buried alongside the ammunition that never made it to war.

I can acknowledge that the security functions of the Department of Defence – a highly sensitive portfolio – would pose administrative hurdles that even other government agencies would need to jump in order to conduct environmental recovery. But prohibiting access to certain areas triggers suspicions as frightening as the explosive ordinances once manufactured here. What else may have happened in those factories filled with workers possessing little experience, whose bodies did their best to handle pyrotechnic chemicals in the production of nine-inch projectiles and bombs weighing over a hundred kilos?

RESEARCHERS JILL BARNARD, Graeme Butler, Francine Gilfedder and Gary Vines emphasise that 'during World War Two thousands of people worked here on round-the-clock shifts, doing for the most part, very dangerous work'. Other historical reports highlight how the casualty building needed to be extended during the Second World War, doubling in size, allowing for further speculation that injuries were a very real and regular occurrence. Now the military waste is left to desecrate the land, accentuating the horrendous undertaking that occurred there: the risks these workers took making bombs and the possibility that mistreatment, accidents and even death may haunt the site.

Sitting with these thoughts and histories, both known and speculative, I started to imagine holding a bullet in my hand or filling TNT into bombshells – actions that evoke a type of violence I never want to see. I wondered who these factory workers were. And whether the immensity of the Second World War, in a very different political and social era, surpassed any sense of guilt, confusion or grief that someone might experience working in an explosives factory now. Scenarios formed in my imagination, both gruesome and banal, conjuring the boredom of repetitive physical labour in a factory line and the potential consequences if something went wrong.

I narrowly glimpsed small details of these workers' lives in an aural history project curated by the Living Museum of the West. Titled *'Go West, Young Woman!' Munitions Diary 1985*, it features interviews with various women who worked in the factory, as well as in other ammunition production sites in Footscray, Yarraville and Essendon, during the Second World War. Their reflections capture how they worked under conditions 'demanding exactness and imposing danger – not positions of power but of considerable responsibility'. Their accounts are redolent with a distinct oddness and absurdity, a detached honesty that, beyond the petrifying risks they took, demonstrates how deranged and unpleasant it all seemed. One worker, named Alma Taylor, recalled:

> Most of the women up there hadn't done that sort of job, but they all sort of pitched in. It was a bit of a lark when we all built air raid

> shelters. We would've all drowned in them because they all got full of water. But I tell you, I don't think we needed to know where air raid shelters were because if they raided up there we'd all be blown anyway with what they were making.

A Mrs Billie Anderson likewise explained, 'You'd see people going around with their skins all yellow, and you'd know: Well, they were working on such-and-such powder or TNT powder. Made you just go all yellow, you know. Just discoloured you like dye.'

Despite their extraordinarily strange working conditions and surreal tenacity, it was the ordinary fears of these women that left me unsettled. Many described how scared they were to enter and leave factory buildings during night shifts – a concern that still troubles women and gender diverse people navigating public spaces today. These tensions were exacerbated by the US soldier Eddie Leonski, later dubbed the Brownout Strangler, who was deployed to Melbourne during the war and murdered three women in the vicinity. As one of the interviewees, Audrey McMaster, remarked:

> I can remember the night we were on afternoon shift, lined up already to come, waiting for the whistle to blow and the night shift was coming in – 'There's been another girl murdered! There's been another girl murdered!' And we were thinking: 'Oh! We've got to go home and walk in the dark!' And that was Leonski. We were frightened at night.

It's easy to be consumed by the terror of it all, to imagine the worst. It's also easy to assume that the Australian Army and Department of Defence covered up certain incidents – a suppression that may still linger, evident in the difficulty government agencies have experienced accessing certain sections of the site.

The possibility that things were purposely hidden feels even murkier when you consider that the only time the factory openly welcomed people was to mark its fiftieth anniversary on family day in 1960. ABC video footage of the celebration shows neatly dressed women raking gun powder across troughs into shells below with clinical uniformity. The pristine machinery and the focused attention of female staff offer a harmonious image of work on the factory line – a sanitised version of reality at odds with the women's real experiences.

To dwell on this history is important, and it's worthwhile to hold these women's frightening experiences, which are so removed from most of the materials available. But it also obscures the overwhelming splendour I experienced when I first saw the site from Canning Reserve Lookout. The view as I gazed across the river – its vastness and unusual details, mismatched buildings, tunnel networks dug into grass-covered earth mounds and dense shrublands – evoked endless possibilities of what it might be. I thought of co-operative living and refurbishing the deteriorating buildings that still appeared structurally sound. I witnessed its boundlessness, aware that it didn't begin or end within the limits of urban planning or the desire for city dwellers to be ethically housed.

MANY OTHERS ONCE stood on the horseshoe bend of the river, immersed in ceremonial practices. Their story was different – because it had disappeared as much as it still existed. A culture that moves not as a single or definable narrative anymore but that is embodied in new forms along the Maribyrnong that I've traversed compulsively, enamoured by the river's strength and the red gums, bottlebrushes and reed beds that grow along its banks. Feelings that many others held and wanted to protect in ways that almost surprised me.

For First Nations people, relationships to Country have remained as cities have evolved, but the desire from non-Indigenous people to acknowledge, understand and engage with this culture has grown, offering a sense of resolve. In those community engagement summaries, I found that preserving and celebrating Aboriginal culture was highly valued: VicUrban's 2010 engagement offered opportunities to 'ensure Indigenous history and culture of the site is regarded as highly as the defence history'. The VPA's 2018 community workshops similarly highlighted a 'focus on the Indigenous significance of the site and the stories of defence', suggesting that future developments must continue to acknowledge Indigenous culture through signage and educational opportunities.

In many ways, these responses reflect the complex feelings that drew me to the site: shock at the oddity of its defence history; awareness that something far more significant exists; worry that access to unsettling photos of young women smiling at the camera while sorting bullets threatens to overshadow the deeper stories of the Eastern Kulin Nations. Stories that vastly pre-date photography and the dominance of Anglo history. But as I continued to look at these photos, I was reminded of the connections, the brutal messiness of it all, and how I risked analysing these histories incorrectly if I approached them as separate things.

Initially, I searched for pre-colonial stories of the site as if they were more important than the experiences of the Aboriginal people who'd worked there in recent history. I failed to consider the experiences of the Aboriginal women who'd also been employed at the explosives factory during the war. When I read the *Maribyrnong Aboriginal Heritage Study*, commissioned by the local council in 1999, I was reminded of the continuum of culture and the inherent fallacy of history that contains people and events within a linear timeline. The study explicitly detailed the incursion into Country by weapons manufacturing: 'Earlier disturbance to the area caused by farming and grazing would not have been as extensive, but the construction and on-going expansion of the factory since 1910, has had a significant and deleterious impact on any remaining Aboriginal sites in the area.'

This disruption came with myriad ramifications that we struggle to grasp today in our search for ways to address what happened here – while the mainstream consciousness still imagines it should be done via urban tropes like walking tours and signage. But the study demonstrates that culture is not just something to be remembered or preserved. It's persistent and present: 'Silcrete, a type of stone, was also an important resource available to Aboriginal people in the valley. Silcrete was the most widely used stone in the production of tools… Many of these sites remain today, even in developed areas.'

Culture will always remain in the urban environment, a phenomenon that fascinates archaeologists as much it often confounds planners and developers, who are unsure how to protect it even when the desire to celebrate it is strong. But culture is fixed in the survivance of Aboriginal people, who, as the study also shows, worked in the explosives factory manufacturing bullets alongside the other workers who are far more visible: the white women who regularly appear in photos from national archives or televised news reports of the family day.

While details about Aboriginal workers at Maribyrnong are limited, I was struck by the experience of Margaret Tucker, a Yorta Yorta woman, activist and writer whose autobiography, *If Everyone Cared Enough: Her Voice Reclaimed*, was one of the first memoirs written by an Aboriginal woman, published in 1977. In it, she describes her experience at the explosives factory with a gracious fortitude that defies the violence germane to the role:

> I liked working there; there was a lovely big canteen with a stage and music. But I shuddered at the bullets that were being made. I was on the machines. I liked working machines. On night shift to stop going to sleep while we worked, we would start singing till the whole works were joining in. I couldn't help myself; I loved singing and would go for my life on the high notes.

And while she shuddered at what passed through her hands, I was moved by her voice, her desire to sing, leading a chorus to stay awake as they worked through the night. There was a stoic power in her actions compared with the other women's reflections I'd read. Amid the chaos, pressure, danger and uncanny predicaments they endured, she remembered the music and the possibility of joy within horror.

Strangely, her desire to sing reminded me of another observation documented in the Aboriginal Heritage study – a crude account from the diary of a settler who described the area in the 1840s: 'Aborigines were everywhere, and the nights were split asunder by the sound of corroborees and fights between rival tribes. Nearly every night a corroboree was gone through with all its grotesque and barbaric accompaniments of music, beaten by the lubras on possum rugs, and the songs of excitement.'

I will never be able to hear these 'barbaric accompaniments of music' – songs so powerful it's almost reasonable that a settler would interpret them as 'grotesque', unable to comprehend the vast rhythms of a culture that eclipsed the rigidity of his own British lineage. But these 'songs of excitement' were passed down. They moved through time, misinterpreted and degraded but echoing on in other incarnations. Carrying through the voices of women like Margaret Tucker, who sang to make her circumstances bearable. A song to soothe the harsh touch of weapons and acknowledge the much larger wars that occurred on her Country.

IT'S DIFFICULT TO know how to honour stories about a site that remains vacant, its future as unanswerable as the past we can't reconcile. In community meetings, well-meaning locals asked that we celebrate both histories, as if they are two different things, while the cost of environmental remediation inhibits both government and the private sector from doing anything. And the site remains silent, unable to articulate what happened or how to move on.

A 2025 update from the Department of Defence feels hushed and opaque: a vague statement on their website telling us how it's currently assessing 'open market tenders to determine a cost-effective solution for the remediation and future redevelopment options of the site'. And the process repeats itself. As if to taunt us, reinforcing the site's desertion and the stories that remain unanswered, scattered across a multitude of documents that are difficult to access and frustratingly scarce when found.

The cost to remediate seems lighter now, a reasonable figure in comparison to the heaviness of history embedded within its grounds. A sum of money like any other item of government expenditure listed in federal budgets by an exorbitantly wealthy nation that can spend $18 billion on AUKUS but not $200 million to clean explosive residue that seeps through the soil. A military detritus left uncleared, delaying vital housing, amenities, jobs and even small answers to our collective grief. And as these urban problems proliferate, there's a part of me that wants only to know if the women got home safely, if the workers recovered from the accidents that occurred when they handled pyrotechnics, and the courage the Kulin Nations displayed during our own frontier wars. But mostly I imagine the sound of Margaret Tucker's voice echoing across the landscape almost a hundred years later, still hitting those high notes with aplomb.

Timmah Ball is a writer and urban planner of Ballardong Noongar heritage. In 2022, she published the chapbook *Do Planners Dream of Electric Trees?* through Glom Press, and her work has appeared in publications such as *This All Come Back Now* (UQP) and *Best Australia Poems* (Australian Poetry), both 2022.

FICTION

This is my life

Daniel Ray

QUINN'S ON THE porch. I can see him over Mum's shoulder through the smudged vertical strip of glass next to the front door. Golden porchlights flicker and zip with midges and moths. Occasionally, his shifting shadow cuts off the light. I'm sitting with Mum and Dad at the dinner table. We finished eating an hour ago and are barely talking. We're drinking and waiting for him. Red wine furs my tongue. The room's too hot, air jetting from the ceiling ducts, and smells of meat and salt. Crickets drone, punctuated by the sudden, dropping *bonks* of frogs. I wonder what would happen if I were to say: 'He's standing there, outside.' But I want to give him more time to savour the cold, to slip on a second skin.

The table's bone-coloured with a burnished steel frame. Mum bought it around three years ago after Dad got his new job. I think she still feels guilty about the cost, even though we have plenty of money. Sometimes she rubs its leg like it's a dog. Opposite me is a crystal vase with faceted edges. Hyacinths droop over its flared rim. Their stems look like fleshy specimens in a greenish solution. Mum makes us keep flowers until they're long dead, as if she wants to squeeze every last drop of beauty out of them. I hate watching the flowers shrivel, brown, rot, turn inwards on themselves. It's worse when they bloat: colours blooming from petal tips then changing all at once like a gas flame suddenly overtaken from orange to blue. When I can't take it anymore, even though Mum complains later, I sneak them onto the compost pile, trying not to look at their skeletons.

Dad drums the table. He used to play the piano when he was younger. He's mostly clumsy. Mum often shouts, 'Get the Betadine!' because he's tripped on the porch, fallen into a ditch, cut himself chopping tomatoes, raked his arm through a blackberry bush, lodged a splinter deep in his palm. I like watching Mum tend to him, thick fingers calloused and steady, looking more like a priest than a nurse: hovering a needle over a candle flame and anointing him with burnt orange. It's only when there's an afterimage of Dad's music, when he does something like the drumming, or mimics a bird call – eyes narrowed while he zeroes in on the intonation – that he's almost graceful.

Mum purses her lips and absently swirls the wine in her glass. It's past nine and there's only another hour or so until this all falls apart. Each night, as soon as I sit at the dinner table, I can see the future as if I'm watching a scene in a film where a car slices down a stretch of road, the sky a cloying sheet of grey filled with slanting bars of rain, and I know there's about to be a crash that's been set in motion long before this.

Even when you know something will happen, you don't know precisely what will cause it or how its *happening* will play out. Every moment gives in to a new moment: a chain where each link slides indiscernibly into the next. My perception of the evenings actually starts before then, when the bottle of white wine is pulled from the fridge and cracked open after the dinner preparations have begun: onions sautéing, meat browning, potatoes wet and pale. Or does it start even earlier than that? When I hear Mum's clicking shoes on the path and some part of me measures the weight of her steps, the smoothness of her gait, how slickly the key slides into the front door? All this to ascertain what sort of mood she's in and how much she will drink.

A triple rap on the door makes me jump in my chair.

'Finally,' Dad says.

'Come in!' Mum yells. She's obsessed with locking up the house except when Quinn is coming.

Dad checks his watch. 'He's so late.'

Mum hushes him. 'We're lucky he visits us at all.'

Quinn calls out hello and comes through the dining/television room, past the slumped green couch. A haircut, too sharp, makes his head seem blockier, eyes small, opaque stones. He cradles a bottle of red wine, the usual peace offering, although I've tried to talk him out of it before. Behind him, the white curtain hardly holds out the night.

He moves into the kitchen and looks at us over the bench. Then he grins, almost self-consciously, and says hello again. Dad's smiling and Mum's out of her seat and moving to him. Quinn's gaze roves past mine, barely pausing. But I know we'll catch up later when we're alone. For now, he needs to placate our parents. I warned him yesterday they were angry because he hadn't called or visited in two months. He texted back: *Oh, okay.* Mum gives him a hug and a kiss on the cheek as she says it's so good to see him and that we missed him ('Me too,' he says, almost convincingly) and how nice his woollen coat is (he names an expensive brand). Dad asks him how uni's going. I zone out.

Quinn's studying law at a big uni in a big city three hours north-east of here by car. I've visited him twice. The first time he came to see us for a day then drove back up, and we blared LANKS and Big Scary and Ngaiire with the windows down, wind ruffling our hair and frilling our ears. He pulled over into the lookout at the lake that's mostly dust and grass, and he pointed out the silver bar of water distilled under the horizon. I wanted to touch its pure, cold ingot to my lips.

He took me straight to the campus, which had sandstone buildings that glowed and was scattered with jacaranda trees. He'd sent me photos of their lavender petals bruising the paths in summer, but they were gnarled and bare. Nearly everyone was dressed in black puffer jackets. Boys clopped around in too-shiny RMs, girls in Vans or Docs. I wanted to leave as soon as I arrived. The whole thing seemed part of some unspoken conspiracy to provide the campus with an air of eloquence, erudition, money, class.

'Let me take this.' Mum grabs the bottle of wine by the neck from Quinn, briefly inspecting the label.

'It's a new grenache. I don't think you've tried it.'

'Yum, thank you.'

I remember how last week Dad took me to the grog shop after the supermarket, and we checked out in front of a grizzled man holding a slab of VB. Our trolley clinked with twelve bottles of wine, and Dad gently took them out one at a time, sliding them to the cashier. The price ended up at nearly four hundred bucks and I was embarrassed.

'Quite a selection you've got there,' the man said.

Dad turned. 'Well, you get bored otherwise.'

The man nodded and smiled with one corner of his mouth, eyes glittering darkly. 'That's true. You wouldn't be able add mine to that, would you?' Dad half-chuckled and went to pay. My body sweated and shivered.

Mum is telling Quinn how she cleaned his room. 'And I made up your bed for you.'

It's as though she thinks that if she's the perfect host, there's a chance he'll decide to stay with us for good, move all his stuff back (the green lamp, the antique bedside table) and fill the main bathroom with the blue-domed bottles of deodorant he buys in bulk, transfer his degree to a closer city.

'Oh. You didn't have to.'

'I wanted to.'

TODAY MUM ASKED us four times how long we thought Quinn's drive would be and when we thought he was leaving so she 'had time to prepare'. Quinn never texts when he's on the way. The day before he leaves, he sends a time he'll arrive 'give or take' a few hours. His nickname in our Messenger chat is ~. Often, he seems to show up from nowhere like an angel who's been vaguely prophesied.

Mum is standing too close, looking up at his face. His eyes are fixed on a point over her shoulder. 'How was the drive?' she asks.

'There was an…accident on the highway.'

Mum makes a small noise and places a hand on Quinn's waist. He looks embarrassed but doesn't shrug her away.

'Nobody was hurt. I think. Just the traffic was bad. Then it got dark early. But I like driving at night.'

'What kind of accident?' Mum asks at the same time Dad says: 'If you'd left earlier, you'd have got here before it was dark.'

Quinn pretends not to have heard him. Dad's face is impassive. He takes another sip of wine then licks his lips, tongue flat and wide.

'Someone got rear-ended or something.'

'Well, we're glad you're here safe,' Mum says. 'It's dangerous with all the trucks whizzing past like maniacs.'

'It wasn't too bad.'

'The truckies are all on amphetamines,' Dad says.

Mum rants about the state of drug use in this country: you can't walk through town or even the city centre without being harassed by a druggie; those two teens stabbed that nice man working at the servo when they were coming down from ice, although at least it wasn't a terrorist attack.

There's no point arguing with her because that's probably what she wants. Quinn sweeps his gaze over the table. I give him a wave, and he flashes a smile before his face goes blank again. He's analysing the state of dinner: our plates empty except for the glimmer of oil and half-chewed pieces of gristle and white lumps of fat; two bottles of wine; our glasses smeared with fingerprints and lip gloss. He's calculating how long he has until the next movement of the evening begins. Mum's a little unsteady and her eyes are glazed. She's talking about Mrs-Robinson-From-Down-The-Road's son, who moved west and got addicted to heroin and no longer talks to her, only sends demands for money through PayPal. Her words are clumsy, misshapen, and she needs to wrangle them into place. My head buzzes from the wine. Eventually, Mum stumbles into silence.

'How was everyone's Saturday?' Quinn asks. I shrug. I know I should be grateful for his attempts to steer the conversation, to minimise the silences and make Mum and Dad happy, but I feel a flash of anger that he's escaped from all this, that he can come back home three or four times a year and pretend that everything is normal and fine.

'I did some gardening,' Dad says.

He works in the garden most weekends. We don't live in the suburban-Gothic part of town with the weatherboarded houses topped with tin roofs and patches of gravel for front gardens. Our block is large and bushy, filled with wattles and their thousand tiny starbursts and the twisting silver ghosts of eucalypts. It's choked with weeds. Patches of stinging nettle. Sticky weed that griddle-marks your skin. Paterson's curse bearing its purple trumpets. What Dad calls *trigger weed*, which spits milky seeds when you brush against them. We have a small dam that changes colour depending on the weather, encircled by bulrushes. Quinn and I used to break off their corndog heads and whack each other until they dissolved into fluff. Up close, the dam's surface is patterned from lurking silt-glossed branches. Dad says this is 'a perfect way to drown'. He used to get angry when our old neighbours' kids went skinny dipping in it at night. They couldn't swim in their own dam because of algae. I remember going outside one evening to see pine trees burning and the water on fire so you could hardly tell the difference between flames and their reflections, and Katy running out with her arms in the air, yelling: 'What the fucking fuck are you doing, Steve?' Steve, who'd poured gasoline into their dam and spent the next four months regrowing his eyebrows.

Now Quinn's saying: 'What's for dinner? Sorry I'm late.'

'Roast lamb,' Dad says.

'That's okay.' Mum gestures messily in the direction of the microwave. 'We left a plate for you.'

I hate roasts. Dad patrols the kitchen, tea towel draped over his shoulder, a wooden spoon aloft, checking the meat to see if it needs turning or more liquid added. After it's rested, he takes a sleek carving knife and a honing steel and whets the knife with a *shing-shing-shing*. He's taught me this action doesn't technically sharpen the blade but makes it keen. Is that what happens before you enter heaven? Does God glide a finger up and down your soul until it seems thin enough to slip between atoms? Until it sings? Dad carves the meat, squinting over his rimless glasses that fog up from the heat, looking directly into each cut. It feels as if he's copying a performance, a ritual, he learnt from his dad, who learnt it from his dad (and on and on) about the *proper duties* of The Patriarch.

Sometimes when my parents make me trim the fat from chicken or veal, or slice hormone-enlarged chicken breasts into thin slices, I feel pain in my forearm or thigh as if I'm cutting myself. Maybe I'll become a vegetarian once I move out of here and I have some of my own money, although I'd need a job first. I'm thinking of going as far south as I can. I want to be away from the dust, the dry air, the heavy sun, the shouting.

MUM COMES BACK to the table with a glass for Quinn. He's gone to use the bathroom and put his stuff in his room. She takes a sip of wine, sets the glass down gently and strokes a thumb over its foot as if she's a potter moulding it to the table.

'He's looking a little thin,' she says.

'I don't think he's getting enough sleep,' Dad says.

'Too much on his plate.'

'In the microwave?' I joke, but they ignore me.

'They work the students hard.' Dad divvies up the rest of the bottle. His lips look bloodless. Mum watches him carefully as if making sure he doesn't sneak an extra drop for himself, shadows flaring in her eye sockets. 'Well, that's all of it,' he says.

'Nothing in the cellar?' Mum finishes the glass. I watch her throat move as she swallows.

'Nothing cheap.'

'Just drink the exy stuff,' I say.

Dad looks at me flatly. 'It's ageing.'

'Lucky Quinn brought a bottle,' Mum says and grabs it from the kitchen. It's a screw-top and she opens and pours it. Some spills over the neck and she licks it off. 'We'll buy some more tomorrow.'

'He likes being busy,' I say.

'I wonder where he gets that from,' Mum says drily, looking at Dad.

Dad laughs. 'You can talk.'

I tip back the rest of my wine. 'Maybe it's your shared genetics.'

I shake my head when Mum goes to pour me more from Quinn's bottle.

Her eyes flash almost yellow. 'If it is, they've skipped you. What did you do today?'

'Not much.'

'Have you thought about a job?' Dad says.

'You can always go back to uni next semester,' Mum says.

'Sure. You just need to do something now.' I can tell Dad has tried to say this as gently as he can, but there's a sourness that's kept growing in the months after I dropped out of my online uni courses in week three.

I am doing *something*. Addy, Bel and I break into houses during the day, when it's most dangerous and we get the biggest rush – although we make sure the cars are gone and no one's at home. We make sandwiches with whatever's available and drink milk straight from the bottle and sit on fuzzy rugs, trading sidelong glances with suspicious calico cats. Thursday, after Quinn leaves, we have plans for a sprawling pseudo-mansion on the edge of town. Addy and Bel have scoped it out. Maybe they'll have a sex dungeon. The owners' cars have been gone for a week and mail is piling up in the letterbox. I wonder if the door's locked, if we'll have to break a window. I want to see

Addy throw a rock through it, his body extending, rippling with movement; I want to hear him cry out when it smashes.

Quinn's hanging back in the kitchen doorway next to the fridge. He rolls his eyes at me, which makes me grin. I hide it by scratching my lip.

'This is fucking serious, Jem!' Mum yells. 'This is your life.'

LATER, MUCH LATER, after the shouting stops and Mum has left a half-drunk glass of red wine on the bench skinned in Glad Wrap, I go to Quinn. The house is quiet except for the *shhh (shhh) (shhh)* of wind. I tap on his door and open it. He glances up from his laptop, hunched and tired. I give a small gesture with my thumb. He nods and puts on his shoes, and we go outside for a smoke, propping the front door open so it doesn't make any noise. For a long time, we shiver in silence. I like the burn in my throat, how the air mixes with the smoke. We stand in the cold dark, cigarette tips gleaming, smoke curling and coiling trancelike.

'Mum's…' He trails off.

'Yeah.'

'On the boooooze.' I think it's meant to be funny but neither of us laughs. He takes a long drag. 'Is it like this –'

'Yep.'

'Every night?' His voice is more resigned than curious.

'Pretty much.'

He sighs. 'Not good.'

I feel a surge of bitterness and scuff a foot on the porch. 'At least you haven't had to deal with it.'

He's looking at me over the top of his glasses. His nose wrinkles a bit, which it does when he's sincere or thinks he's right. 'That's why I moved away.'

'You should call them more often. She gets upset. It's worse when she's upset.'

He sighs. 'I know, I know.' There's a pause. 'Maybe you should leave, too.'

'Money…'

Quinn's face is grey in the darkness. 'You need to move out eventually. I can help a bit.'

A long silence until an owl hoots. The sound burrows into my chest and stays there, echoing. Quinn crouches down and stubs out the cigarette, then picks it up delicately with two fingers. We'll need to sneak them into the bin later. Mum doesn't know we smoke.

'Christmas.'

'What?' Quinn says.

'By Christmas.' My mouth is suddenly dry, and my head spins from the nicotine. 'I'll move out by Christmas.'

Daniel Ray lives between Naarm and Queanbeyan. His writing is published in *Meanjin*, *Griffith Review*, *Short Fiction*, *Island* and elsewhere. He was shortlisted for the 2023 and 2024 Griffith Review Emerging Voices competitions. He is currently writing his debut novel, supported by a Create NSW grant. Daniel is a PhD student at La Trobe University, researching queerness and affect.

Merinda Dutton

Hello weary traveller

your coming was whispered to me, long-long ago
my heart warms and sizzles
to have you folded at my roots
your arrival here was written
when supernovas were waiting to be born
which is to say, Ocean planned our symphony
and Sky dreamt of many epochs like this one
gather lemon myrtle leaves, bub!
brew us a tea
we have much to converse on
the moment has come for you to rest
i know you are weary, and your spirit is tired
rest as long as you need, my love
lay your body down
allow Earth's breath
to fill your blood until you are nourished
rest for the time it takes
a river to fill its banks
when you wake, take a deep breath
breathe in Sky
until your lungs are all but the milky way
stretch your limbs
i sense your legs are heavy
i know you carry leaden worries in your heart
you have walked many frontiers
i hear your bones aching
breathe all the way out

let your lungs untangle
and breathe Sky back in
rest more if your skin tells you so
perhaps when you are replenished
you'll grant me a song and dance
i know of a grass circle nearby
that would welcome your feet
stay here as long as there is magic
to be found in the moon
stay here
and we will speak love words in the quiet
dusk's birdsong marks a new season
yesterday's ember holds archives
for tomorrow's fire
and today the hush of smoke
gifts us a story
of now

Merinda Dutton is a Barkandji and Gumbaynggirr woman, mother, lawyer and co-founder of Blackfulla Bookclub on Instagram. Her creative practice explores kinship, Country and justice through poetry and storytelling. Her work has appeared in *Sydney Review of Books*, *Griffith Review*, *Australian Poetry Journal* and *The Suburban Review*, and she contributed to the anthology *Words to Sing the World Alive* (UQP, 2025).

NON-FICTION

Noticing teeth

On dentistry, poverty and the ethics of ethnography

Eve Vincent

I INTERVIEWED ELISABETH outside the bakery. As part of the research for my 2023 book, *Who Cares? Life on Welfare in Australia*, I was talking to people subject to the first trial of the cashless debit card. The card sequestered 80 per cent of social security payments onto a card that was linked to the EFTPOS system and could not be used to purchase alcohol or gambling products. The remaining 20 per cent of a recipient's income support was paid into their bank account and could be withdrawn as cash. In Ceduna, South Australia, where I met Elisabeth, the card was introduced in 2016. This particular policy experiment in compulsory income management ended in 2022, after the election of the first Albanese government, but other forms of compulsory income management remain in place.

Elisabeth talked of her childhood: her mum and dad were 'always on the road, lookin' for work, work, work'. They were, in effect, Aboriginal itinerant workers in the rural economy, a common experience of the 1960s and '70s in this region. Elisabeth's sisters 'stepped upwards', often taking care of her. Elisabeth told me the cashless debit card 'caused [her] embarrassment'.

We'd been talking for almost an hour when she complained, jokingly, that so much talking had made her teeth hurt. That's when I noticed them. Glossy, almost silky. They shone. She said aloud what I was realising: 'They're false!'

From that point on, I started to really notice people's teeth.

Jutting teeth.
A tooth caramel brown and black at the roots, gleaming white at the ends.
Stained, the colour of turmeric or weak tea.

MANY THINGS WERE shared with me while I conducted research into people's experiences of the cashless debit card: a spare bed, a bike helmet, a car filled with dog hair. Anthropologists' dependency on their hosts is a deeper matter still. People entrusted me with their life stories, fears and ideas, some urging me to pass their opinions 'back', 'write a submission to cancel it' or 'put it through' to 'government', others hoping I would help 'get the story out there' to a wider public. My role comes with significant responsibilities: how to act as an ethical witness? How to get these lives down on the page without exploiting them and without causing embarrassment, as Elisabeth might put it?

I sought to write with immediacy about life on welfare. I took inspiration from a passage by writer Maria Tumarkin, who describes how poor people's lives are lived out 'on a highway where they are repeatedly hit by passing trucks'. She continues: 'As they are bandaging their wounds, cleaning them out with rainwater, putting bones back into sockets, another truck's oncoming… Most people have a truck going over them at some period of their life. But on a highway you don't get one or two. You get a convoy. They don't stop. That's the point. The recurrence is the point.'

Perhaps this metaphor grabbed me because I thought of a mate's dad, struck and killed by a truck as he walked home along a poorly lit, often-trod road on the scrubby outskirts of Ceduna. I also admired and hoped to share in Tumarkin's search for a way to energise my writing about difficult lives, avoiding the deadening effects of social science verbiage and instead conveying jaggedness, a quality of existence liable to constant disruptions, both dramatic and everyday. I wanted to capture a kind of jumpiness that I encountered in many of my interlocutors, some of whom twitched with 'stress', as one interviewee emphasised on the numerous occasions I recorded his stories.

My book includes people's voices when they narrate, opine and analyse, when they share with great poignancy, but also when they swear, joke, mangle grammar, elaborate fanciful theories, when they are racist. I'm not willing to suggest that a condition of entitlement to social assistance and care is moral goodness. But to what end? I remain unresolved about the risk of my writing exposing people – although of course my interviewees checked their transcripts and made their own use of me as a resource and as a conduit to readers and the policy process. But I ended up cutting from the manuscript my observations about teeth, among other vignettes that felt doubly exposing: of my research participants and of me.

The sociologist Emma Mitchell has shown that narrating one's 'vulnerability' is key to securing the stingy resources of Australia's welfare state, which has always narrowly targeted spending and is now best understood as highly conditional: 'Conditional welfare requires benefit claimants to routinely make a case for their poverty and to prove that they are both in need and deserving of support,' Mitchell explains.

In her excellent 2023 book, *Making a Life on Mean Welfare*, Mitchell's research participants – people subsisting on income support payments in South Western Sydney – are aware of the need to offer their caseworkers the 'right blend of misfortune and fortitude, deference and resolve'. Some shared with her that telling their caseworker 'everything' had been 'validating'. For others, the demands of this performance of hardship represented another of poverty's tolls, and they resented the intrusion.

To have one's physical and psychic vulnerability set down on the page by a sympathetic but socially powerful scholarly narrator is another matter again. It might insult or shame; in turn, that shame will infect, becoming mine. My task, as I saw it, was to try to grasp, honour and dignify other people's realities, not to aestheticise the evidence of their profound structural subjugation. To avoid ugliness and agonies altogether, however, so as not to risk offence, felt just as ethically compromising.

This is an old debate. In the mid-1980s, anthropologist Philippe Bourgois conducted research among the most socially marginalised denizens of East Harlem. In the introduction to his classic 1995 ethnography, *In Search of Respect: Selling Crack in El Barrio*, he worried about his part in creating and circulating another bad image of the poor. 'At the same time,' he insisted, 'countering traditional moralistic biases and middle-class hostility toward the poor should not come at the cost of sanitizing the suffering and destruction that exists on inner-city streets.' He concluded that glossing over the 'social misery' he'd witnessed would make him complicit in oppression, since the phenomena he presented were symptoms of larger structural inequities and not exposés of bad behaviour.

She has 'ice teeth': no front teeth.

A friend had some teeth screwed in. A screw falls out. She cups one cheek in her palm, her face twisted into a grimace.

I bring soft fruit with me to visit people at home: nectarines, grapes.

TEETH ARE ONE of the most visible markers of poverty: structural circumstances that are individually borne. In an essay for *Aeon*, US journalist Sarah Smarsh calls them 'poor teeth'. She writes: 'Often, bad teeth are blamed solely on the habits and choices of their owners, and for the poor therein lies an undue shaming.' And: 'Poor teeth…beget not just shame but more poorness: people with bad teeth have a harder time getting jobs and other opportunities.' In the age of 'whitened, straightened, veneered smiles', the distance between ruined poor teeth and healthy, wealthy teeth is growing.

In 1970s Australia, when Medicare's predecessor was designed, dental care was left out. Since 2014, the Child Dental Benefits Schedule has enabled children up to seventeen years of age to access free dental care at most private clinics if they're eligible for Medicare and part of a family that receives certain Australian Government payments. 'Dental into Medicare' was a key Greens policy in the 2025 federal election campaign. While this commitment to expanded coverage has stimulated public attention to the question of teeth and poverty in recent years, Grattan Institute researchers stated in late 2024 that 'more than two million Australians avoid dental care because of the cost' and that 'more than four in ten adults usually wait more than a year before seeing a dental professional'. Peter Breadon, the institute's health program director, argues that Australia's public dental system is 'underfunded' and 'overwhelmed'.

In July 2025, the ABC reported that around a third of Australians are eligible for free or low-cost public dental services. These services receive some Commonwealth funding but are provided by state and territory governments. The ABC obtained data showing that while average wait time varies across states and territories, in some cases people have waited years to access dental care.

Left untreated, dental emergencies can result in hospital visits. Or worse. The UK's intensely conditional welfare system imposes a strict Work Capability Assessment in a bid to limit access to disability benefits, as does Australia's through a similar assessment tool. A recent book memorialising the victims of the UK system includes details of a fifty-seven-year-old man found dead in his flat. His relatives discovered the lid of a shoebox in his cupboard holding two large molars and a pair of pliers.

I go on a long drive west, moving past desiccated, yellowing paddocks. Gina regales me with a detailed story about having her false teeth made and tries to explain to me that hers were subsidised by Medicare…or something like that… I doze in the heat, flies buzz about the windscreen. But anyway, it hurts to wear them, her story concludes. She goes without.

On another day, I buy Gina a curry beef pie at the bakery. We sit outside, her chewing cheerfully, gummily, on the soft pastry and meat.

PUBLISHED IN 2014, Linda Tirado's *Hand to Mouth* documents her experiences of being poor, working low-wage, unstable jobs and raising her two children with her husband, who shares her precarious position in the American labour market. In a voice that is direct, sassy, frustrated and funny, Tirado writes about the sex lives of poor people, the costly burdens of poverty (such as late payment fees), her coping mechanisms, the enjoyment she derives from smoking – and about teeth. The book's title has a clever double meaning: it's about how fragile day-by-day existence is but also speaks to the shame surrounding poor teeth, which a hand shielding the mouth attempts to hide.

Tirado's book began life as a post on an online forum she was reading to unwind after a 'particularly gruelling shift' at one of her two jobs. Someone posted the question *Why do poor people do things that seem so self-destructive?* Tirado's extended response went viral; eventually, she was approached to write a book.

The late Barbara Ehrenreich supplied a short, generous foreword. She declared herself 'waiting for this book' since the publication of her 2001 classic, *Nickel and Dimed*. Ehrenreich contrasted her 'brief attempt' to subsist on low-wage service and retail jobs with Tirado's authentic dispatches from impoverished America, lending weight to the valorisation of experiential accounts of poverty over journalistic or scholarly perspectives. Increasingly, people in poverty have challenged the presumption of academics and community sector advocates to mediate their perspectives, using digital platforms, social media accounts and publishing ventures to communicate their direct experiences, embedded knowledges and political demands directly to audiences. The persistent ethical dilemmas anthropologists and journalists must wrestle with, in terms of representing others' lives, have become more heightened still. Ehrenreich declared herself an outsider to the topic of contemporary poverty, Tirado the 'real thing'. She concluded in her foreword, 'But let me get out of the way now. She can tell this story better than I can.'

This is also the premise of the recent Australian collection *Povo* (2024). The storytellers in this book found their voices in workshops run across Western Sydney by Sweatshop Literacy Movement, and they write from direct experience. Teeth are central to one especially compelling contribution. Plot twist! Victor Guan Yi Zhou's story revolves around the narrator's tooth gems, which he takes every opportunity to flash. 'Got them at a salon…right after Mum and Dad kicked me out. Four of them. Two on the top canines. Two on each incisor. Crystal Swarovski. $150 all up. Each gem will help me manifest my dreams.'

A broken-off corner.

I notice teeth missing. Rows like crooked fence posts hammered in hurriedly. Or, just a couple knocked out. One here, one there.

IN THE LEAD-UP to the 2023 Budget, I attended a protest at Albanese's electoral office. I went in solidarity: the protest was organised by the Australian Unemployed Workers' Union. Speakers addressing the protest were on JobSeeker and the Disability Support Pension. They described their struggles to exist on miserly income support payments and shared their frustration about the hope Albanese's election seemed at first to represent – hope that was by then fading. Advocates agree there's been no appreciable rise to the JobSeeker rate for over twenty years now.

There was nervousness, anger, a feeling of betrayal and real desperation in the air; there was also warmth, a sense of community and lashings of grim humour. One single mum wore a T-shirt with this slogan: *I am contributing to society by not raising a dickhead.*

At this protest, I met a JobSeeker recipient who was probably in her late fifties, early sixties. Fraser-era hostility to 'dole bludgers' in Australia revolved around a masculine image of work-shy youth. Today, researchers describe a

JobSeeker recipient as 'likely to be older, to be a woman and importantly to have…a chronic illness or disabilities'. I chatted with this woman about the two days a week she spends kneeling in the bush, tugging out weeds to fulfil her 'mutual obligations', the signature measure of the conditional welfare state. I liked her hand-painted sign, *welfare not warefare*, and took a photo.

In the picture, her mouth is clamped tight. I admit I had noticed her chipped teeth.

Eve Vincent is an Associate Professor of Anthropology in the School of Communication, Society and Culture at Macquarie University. Her books include *Who Cares? Life on Welfare in Australia* (MUP, 2023) and *Love Across Class* (with Rose Butler, MUP, 2024).

NON-FICTION

Disturbing affections

An account in three parts

Emma Maguire

PART I: POSSESSIVE RELATIONS

Acquisition. In the movie *American Psycho*, the main character, Patrick Bateman – a yuppie serial killer with a passion for brutality – is in a nightclub picking up girls with his corporate finance buddies. A girl asks him, 'What do you do?', and he replies honestly, 'I'm in murders and executions.' She can't hear him properly over the loud music, assumes he's said 'mergers and acquisitions', and continues to make small talk over drinks.

The scene is funny because Bateman's vicious nature seems wilfully ignored by the girl even though he makes no attempt to hide it. Sociopathic brutality hidden behind a veneer of expensive commodities: in the movie, this kind of disguise has become the norm in the soulless corporate '80s of Reagan, and Bateman fits in perfectly. The world is shallow and hollow. So is he.

It's become popular to say, 'When people show you who they are, believe them', as if so-called toxic people are easy to detect if we just pay close enough attention. Perhaps this mindset is an antidote or corrective for 'in-group bias', where we extend social graces much further than we should for those we develop relationships with versus the allowances we're willing to make for others. The trouble, though, is that some people become so adept at hiding in plain sight that it becomes impossible for others to register their actions as anything other than normal or benign. And even when they tell you who they are, it's difficult to hear them over the music.

Money. As a postgraduate student, I went to Canada to speak at a conference, and my husband came, too. In preparation for the trip, we exchanged our Australian dollars for glossy new Canadian notes. We riffled through the bills at home, thrilled by the strange currency.

He put a note to his face and sniffed: 'Do they smell like maple syrup to you?'

I laughed.

But they did smell like syrup, and I realised I'd been thinking the same thing since I opened the plastic package full of money. I hadn't allowed myself to put this thought into words, though, because it seemed unlikely and foolish. By this point, I'd learnt to distrust my instincts, to disown my own perceptions. I'd hold my thoughts back because I couldn't trust they'd be received with anything but ridicule.

Financial control is one of the most common and restrictive forms of coercive control. Often, it materialises as men exerting financial control over their female partners, but it can happen to anyone in any kind of relationship.

Warrant. Good sum, round sum, lump sum.
Bond, bank note, coupon, order.
Credit,   liability.
Drawer,   drawee.
Funny money, bogus money,
debasement, erosion, inflation.

I WAS ALWAYS 'bad with money'. I grew up with very little, and when I got some it never lasted long. I ran up credit card bills and lied about them. I'd pay off a thousand dollars, then next time I got depressed I'd spend twice as much on things that made me feel better for a short time. When I grew suicidal, I'd remind myself I had to hold on to life a bit longer because if I died, my husband would be stuck with my debt, and I didn't want him to pay for my irresponsible spending. He was already paying for so much: our rent, the power bill, dinner when we ate out.

The same year I got a divorce, I got good with money. Really good. Spreadsheets-that-talk-to-each-other good.

Payment/nonpayment. When I was in my twenties, I used to run up late fees at my local video store. I'd borrow five DVDs at a time: horror movies and sci-fi mostly. I found those worlds comforting. Genre so neatly contains the unknown, the strange. Feelings like terror and disgust. It gives monsters a shape and confines them within a plot. These films allow us to encounter anxious feelings at a distance, removed from things in our own lives that frighten us more than a cartoonish slasher villain, the real things we keep hidden under our beds.

IN MY VERY early twenties, I defrauded Centrelink for around two grand over a period of three years. Most fortnights when I had to report my income, I creatively adjusted the earnings from my part-time job, tapping in a fictive figure on my keyboard, both knowing what I was doing and refusing to acknowledge what I was doing. I suspect now that this knowing/unknowing was a way of protecting the idea I had of myself as a good person who did the right thing. And when I kept getting away with it, it gave me the impression I could do this wrong thing and still uphold a favourable idea of myself.

It even allowed me to suggest to myself that maybe this thing wasn't really that wrong at all. All that thinking was done in a murky part of my brain I didn't want to know about (even so, I knew about it). It was only when I eventually received a $2,000 debt notice that I had to confront what I'd been doing. I felt so ashamed and guilty: I couldn't put off adjusting that image of myself anymore, from a righteous person to a tainted person who'd done the wrong thing.

I learnt what it is to know I'd been deceitful – and to know myself *known* as deceitful. I didn't like it, and it had a striking deterrent effect. I didn't enjoy the taste of guilt. I discovered that, for me, it just wasn't worth it. Being 'caught' taught me something. But I wonder what might've happened – who I might've become – if I'd been allowed to get away with it.

Credit/debt. To be in someone's debt is an honest and honourable thing when we're talking in metaphors. To owe a debt to somebody is to acknowledge their investment in, or generosity towards, you. To declare you're indebted to somebody is to thank them for what they gave you. I'm indebted to lots of people, but perhaps to no one more than my ex-husband. Nobody has shaped me – my mind, my thoughts – more than he has. I met him at fifteen, when I was open and malleable. We married when I was twenty-four, divorced when I was thirty-five. He was the rock anchoring me to a life through all those years. I moved out of my parents' home and into a home with him. We raised pets together. He supported me financially through the most difficult thing I'd ever done: my postgraduate education. His support was so solid, so complete, that I thought I couldn't survive without it. Thought I couldn't take care of myself, needed him for that.

To credit somebody with something is an honourable practice, too, one of citation. Giving credit where it's due is a principle I'm bound by as someone who works in the academy.

I AM SIXTEEN. We watch a film where a teenage girl seduces a grown man. I am sixteen. We watch a film where a girl-child, maybe twelve or fourteen, is fucked romantically by a paedophile. I am eighteen. I draw a curtain over our past, as if it never happened. Until I'm twenty-two, and I'm made aware of the search term 'pre-teen Lolitas'. I am twenty-two and unable to speak. I am twenty-two, and I read Nabokov's terrible book in a state of shock: learning, learning (but never knowing). I am twenty-three, on holiday by the pool at the resort. I see long-limbed tweens and feel sick to my stomach as we walk by. I am frozen and unseeing, seeing, unseeing.

I am thirty-eight, and sometimes I still see long-limbed prepubescent girls and feel sick, feel horrified, want to rush them away out of sight. I wonder if this way of seeing will ever leave me.

To be *in credit* means you're owed something. You're ahead, and sometime in the future you can collect on the credit you've accrued.

Price. Everything costs us. Every little thing.

PART II: CONTEMPLATIVE AFFECTIONS

Duty/dereliction of duty. What is my duty, in accounting for the past? I have a duty to truth, but the harder I search for The Truth, the more I believe in *truths*, plural. Whose truth do I have a duty to tell? Is it even possible to tell someone else's truth? I think it's possible and dutiful to try.

IN THE CRIMINAL Law Consolidation Act – the Act that governs criminal law in South Australia – maintaining a sexual relationship with a child is considered even more grievous if the offender is in a position of authority over the child: for example, if the person provides them with religious, sporting, musical or other instruction. This dynamic changes the nature of the crime so significantly that the age at which a victim stops being a 'child' for the purposes of sexual consent is raised by one year to eighteen, the age a person is otherwise deemed legally an adult.

This acknowledgement points to a dereliction of duty – the duty adults have to care for children who are made vulnerable by their naivety about life, about people, and by their trust in grown-ups to know and do the right thing. When an adult who holds authority over children uses that trust and vulnerability to harm instead of care for one of them, even the law recognises the seriousness of the dereliction.

Repute. Reputation is everything.

Serial abusers often cultivate a positive reputation that protects them from suspicion, a smokescreen behind which they can source and groom victims and that fortifies them against any accusations that might slip out. It's because of such skilled impression management we sometimes have trouble believing someone is capable of 'that'. But I'm here to tell you they are. They are capable of that. And worse.

DEFENCE LAWYERS UNDERMINE the reputations of women making legal complaints about sex crimes committed against them as a strategy to protect the accused. I wonder all the time about where we're at with this reality as a culture, and whether we still really believe a woman's choice of outfit or her 'body count' or her status as an ex-wife have anything to do with her ability to distinguish between sexual acts that were consensual and sexual acts that were traumatising and illegal.

Revenge. My ex-husband would imagine all the time that people – his mother, his sister, a colleague, me – were trying to 'get back at' him. Any conflict took on the tone of an attack, and an unfair one at that. I'm not a natural scorekeeper, but I'll admit that when something isn't right, I no longer let it lie. Where I saw myself drawing attention to a transgression of the duty we bore each other, he saw an unjust retaliation: he saw me, I think, as vengeful. I can't say which view is correct. I thought I was trying to hold him to account; he experienced an attack on his liberties.

Revenge is always morally ambiguous, but even more so when it comes to women seeking retribution for gendered violence, even though we have a certain tolerance, an appetite, even, for such stories: *Furiosa*, *The Girl with the Dragon Tattoo*, *Carrie*.

Sometimes it's imagined that women seeking justice for sexual crimes committed against them are vengeful. But, in truth, all most of us want is for men to stop doing it – to us, to other women. To simply stop them from hurting us.

PART III: MORAL SENTIMENTS AND MORAL CONDITIONS

Contempt.

Sent away with a flea in the ear.
Spurn, lick, fling to the wind,
    repudiate.
Scout, flout, hoot, hiss,
a cold shoulder turned upon.
Despised, unrespectable, unworthy,
trampled underfoot.
A dismal collective hiss, the sound of public scorn.
Disdainful, scornful, haughty.

The ditzy girl talking to Patrick Bateman in *American Psycho* presents a dilemma. She's in mortal peril, we understand, but it's all her own fault. If she'd only listened more carefully, paid better attention, she could have run to safety. I don't know if it's my oversensitivity or if the film encourages us to view her with a little contempt.

'In contempt of court' is a courtroom phrase. It makes punishable the act of intervening or meddling in court process and authority. 'Court' is also a word that describes the social process of early dating. To court someone is to woo, seduce or take them out. You might not know that the grooming of minors was initially referred to as 'seduction' by law enforcement prior to the 1970s. Retired FBI agent Kenneth Lanning's article on the history of the term explains that 'acquaintance molesters' (molesters known to the child victim) often use grooming rather than violence to prevent abuse from being detected. They do so because grooming acts to control victims by conditioning them to believe their abuser is a trusted friend, that the abuser cares deeply for them, and to see the abuse as either their own fault or as something it isn't: a love story, a normal part of life, a secret they need to protect.

Account. An account is a place to store money, a container of value. It's also a story of what happened. To account for something is to explain why it happened. Accountability is a measure of responsibility or fault. To be accountable is to be responsible; it is also to be legible. Accounting can be a straightforward process of addition and subtraction, organised by columns. It can also be utterly impossible.

Approbation. I have a lasting habit of seeking approval from my partner, even now – that approval meaning something more than my own desires, my own needs, my own instincts. I crave the relief of approval and fear its opposite. My therapist tells me this impulse is part of a psychological schema caused by the pressure an authority figure exerted during the tender age my brain, my psyche, was forming. Specifically, my psychologist says, it relates to the 'subjugation' schema – my second most dominant schema according to the test results. The handout she gave me describes it like this:

> *Subjugation*: This schema refers to the belief that one must submit to the control of others in order to avoid negative consequences. Often these clients fear that, unless they submit, others will get angry or reject them. Clients who subjugate ignore their own desires and feelings.

Accusation. I struggle to imagine what it feels like to find yourself accused of a crime. Especially when, deep down, you don't view what you did as criminal. When you view yourself as a good guy, or at least a good-enough guy. When you asked her, 'Are you sure you want to do this?' before taking her virginity, even if, unknown to you, she didn't understand that by 'this' you meant 'sex'. When you were so careful to make sure her parents knew about you two, because you were older and she was your student. When you educated her about her body, taught her about sex, and she seemed so willing – at least once you'd broken her in, as girls must be. When, later, after all that, you supported her while she did her PhD. When you never hit her. When you let her pursue the career she wanted, even though it meant she wouldn't earn proper money for another four years, and that put the burden on you. When she started talking back and asking questions, harping, attacking your rights and freedoms, like your right to spend your free time with teenage girls, even though by this stage you were nearing forty. When she seemed to be accusing you of something but wouldn't come out and say it. When you both agreed to end the marriage, and it was amicable and she didn't know yet about your teenage lover. When you had no idea that, later, she started having flashbacks, the past reaching through time to grip her in a cold panic. When you had no idea things were starting to make sense to her, as memories of her body being invaded insisted on being remembered: not in the way she'd half-known so many things before but in a way that demanded the full glare of attention and release. I can't imagine what it must be like to wonder, 'Why is she bringing all of this up now?', to think you'd got away with doing something that might technically be wrong but that for so many years, you'd both agreed was okay.

Even though the law is there in black and white. Even though my body has *kept the score*. Accusing you still feels like an act of betrayal.

Absence or violation of law. I had trouble adjusting to high school. Compared to the safety of primary school, it felt like a lawless place. I missed a lot of school that year. The next year, I missed less school, but I began self-harming. The year after that, I met the man who would become my husband. His job was to teach me how to play music. It would be unfathomable to fifteen-year-old me to imagine that at thirty-eight I would make the conflicted decision to talk to a police officer about what would unfold that summer and the years following it. And that the officer would take it seriously, would call him the word I never could (and still can't).

The absence of law is radically different from the violation of law. What if you're ignorant of the law and don't believe you're breaking it? What if you're wilfully ignorant of the law, and you don't believe you're breaking it but understand that what you're doing with these young girls is probably not approved of by other adults? By most adults, anyway.

There was, after all, that time you saw the IT guy late one night at school, and you both understood what you were doing there but didn't talk openly about it. Even so, he made a dirty joke to you and you laughed uncomfortably. What he probably didn't know was that you wouldn't always go there alone to use the school's internet-connected computer, and that it was in the staff room of that very same school I first saw women on their knees, unclothed, begging, humiliated.

Addendum. When I was fifteen, I won an academic prize and was awarded a book voucher. With it I bought a *Roget's Thesaurus*. Dictionaries had always fascinated me, but when I found the thesaurus, a new world opened up. This was a way of classifying language, organising words and cataloguing their relations, mapping kindnesses and distinctions in the most parsing, nuanced way. Its system opened out worlds of meaning.

When I was fifteen, I met a person who became my world of meaning for nineteen years. At thirty-eight, I began clearing away the clouds that had obscured my past and waking up to the reality of it. Words – and ways of organising them – have been key to my reawakening. I hope now when somebody tells me he is 'in murders and executions', I can hear the difference between the words he says and the synonymy I'd once have perceived to protect myself from the knowledge of his violence.

Author's note: This piece contains remixed excerpts from, and an organisational logic inspired by, The Project Gutenberg eBook of *Roget's Thesaurus*, by Peter Mark Roget. Posting date: 2 March 2011 [ebook #22]. Release date: December 1991. Last updated: 5 January 2004. I want to thank Matilda Bookshop in Stirling, South Australia, for its sponsorship of a school prize that enabled me to obtain my first *Roget's Thesaurus*.

Emma Maguire is an Australian writer working across Tarndanya, Thul Garrie Waja and Gurrimbilbarra. She writes essays, criticism, short fiction and literary scholarship, and she's deputy editor of *Life Writing*. She works at JCU, where she's a slightly disillusioned but dedicated academic. You can find her work and writing at emmamaguire.wordpress.com.

FICTION

Piggy

Victor Guan Yi Zhou

'Yes. Yes. I am ready,' I said. Unsure of what I was getting ready for. Something good. Something inexplicable. Something only now and never again. It was the fire of the final time.

THE WIFE TOOK her sweet time in the ensuite shower.

Outside the bedroom window, on the street, young men hollered past in fast cars. Mutts barked from somewhere beyond.

The bedroom contained a bed and side tables – minor nothings picked out by the wife.

My pants vibrated. It was a quarter past eleven. The wife and I were supposed to be getting ready for bed. But it was P.

He texted: *Keen?*

The shameful warmth in my groin already grown large.

More intense.

P sent a photo. His caramel skin was smooth like acrylic; his arms tanned, amber and thin; his elbows darker, purplish; his waist, petite; and shiny like seal skin was his squeaky-clean butt, spread wide open. At the heart of it, right there, in all its scandal, was the most undignified part of him – a bruised plum-purple star. I wanted to gobble him up. All of him. Make him never exist. Embrace him. Pound him. I whipped out my hard penis, sucked in the flabby belly I'd hated my entire life and snapped a photo.

I texted him: *Look at the horrible things you do to me.*

P was typing. He stopped. A heart reaction. He started typing again. A new message: *Pick me up in an hour?*

When the wife turned off the water, I jammed my penis through the fly of my pants, contorting it down to size, and zipped. She was flapping towels, humming a tune. I locked the phone and shoved it deep into my pocket. When she opened the door, the lights from the bathroom backlit her pregnant body. She looked to me, rested her bare spine along the doorframe, propped a damp foot up for support, and belted out her song into an imaginary microphone: *The only one is you. The only one is you. The only one is you.* She reached out to me, enunciating each syllable, flicking her wet hair across her face, holding her belly big with our child. *The only one is you.*

There was no time for this. On the ground, in pieces, was the unassembled cot. Stowed away in my pocket was P, vibrating. Waiting.

I sat down on the bed, motioning the wife over: 'Come here.'

With her head cocked to one side, she told me to come over there instead. She bit the corner of her mouth, unserious.

'Just come over here,' I said. 'You're all wet and cold. You'll get yourself *and* the baby sick.'

She sighed much too loud, complaining to be heard. 'Do you remember a thing called fun? I don't know if you do, but it's something we used to have.'

'I'm just worried for the baby. And you. Plus, you shouldn't be leaning against the door like that. Do you know how many people break bones or even die from slipping –'

'You're a psycho.' She ripped a towel from the rack and wiped the rest of herself dry. 'You are *so* beyond. Can you just relax? Do you even know how to relax, you jittery freak?' She chucked the towel onto the bathroom floor – the one thing she knew I couldn't stand. 'It's embarrassing, you know? When you just shut me down like that.'

Deep breath in.

I paid for this damned home: full brick with a yard for the chocolate labrador she wanted. *Hold two...three...four.* Long, tedious days reviewing ledgers and balancing budgets and calculating incidental expenses. Work that left me feeling dull and meaningless.

Breath out two...three...four...

I had to. It was for the family. The wife and the baby-to-be. Her name will be Ana. Short for Anastasija, like her baba: a saintly woman who raised three kids on discipline and the Catholic fear of God.

Anastasija... A name befitting even the brightest star.

Stand down. Let the wife ramble, let her tire herself.

She sat on the bed next to me and scrolled away on her phone. There was a video of a baby mashing banana. But the wife jerked her phone away from me.

'Don't feel like showing me?' I asked.

'No.' She licked her minty teeth.

I moved in closer, brushed a strand of wet hair away from her face and behind her ears. 'You're right. I'll leave you alone.' And with this I leant down to give a final kiss to her swollen belly.

'I swear... Don't do that ever again. Don't shoot me down like that. You're not my father. You're my *partner*,' she said.

'You're right, babe. I'm sorry. I'll do better next time.'

She let out a sigh and put her earphones in.

'Love you,' I said. Two perfect words to punctuate the end of a fight, to reset. Words to feed a family. 'Love you,' I repeated, louder this time, more sing-song. I needed to hear it from her.

'Isn't it time for you to shower?' she said. Her back was to me.

I WASHED MYSELF with her rose-scented cleanser. I scrubbed my face and then my pits, eventually placing the bottle back on the rack and using a bar of soap instead. A mental video of the wife licking P with the full length of her tongue shook me, killed some small part of me. I couldn't use her cleanser for him. It was a gift from her friends for our housewarming. I washed myself again, twice over with foamy soap, running my hands along my body.

P was amateur when I first met him: after introductions, he closed his eyes, tensed his neck, and puckered his gob like some sort of receptacle. I held his shoulder and gave him a doting look. *You're safe with me.* Over months, we both learnt more about his body and mine. His kisses became less tense, more relaxed. He knew where I liked it, and I found where he liked me. Now, as the wife's nine months were ending, I grew more desperate for his body, more rushed. Peeling back my foreskin, I carefully washed between myself until I smelled of nothing. This will be the last time. The *very* last time. I made a pact with myself. I would break it off with him tonight.

I rushed out of the bathroom. 'Sorry, babe!' I resisted the urge to look away from her eyes. She stopped rubbing her belly to take out her earphones.

I pointed to the phone I was holding pointlessly against my ear. 'It's work again.' She plugged her earphones back in. I scrambled into the closet, where I put on some smart-looking khakis and a cotton T-shirt.

When I jumped into my white Tesla, I felt that blunt gut-punch feeling I sometimes got. I slid off my ring and dropped it in the glove box.

I WAS NUDGING the speed limit, testing how fast I could go. Driving southbound on Old Northern Road and passing overhead powerlines to reach Windsor Road, two hands on the wheel – blood pulsing, face throbbing, focused – I was reminded of my very first attempt at Sydney Park. It was a different Asian boy. Before P. Even before the wife.

There had been mountainous shapes in the distance, verdant indigo in the setting sun. The smell of still pond water and rained-on grass. Shadows of possums, staring. Moon along the horizon. Cave-dark bushes to hide behind. The huge expanse above. The starless sky stretching open the mind. The anticipation of ecstasy as I walked deeper into the bushes. The horrible pain in my stomach. *What if I'm not going to be able to get it up? What if I'm caught? It won't be worth it. No – but it will, for a moment.*

Before I could message *I'm here* on the app – there on a eucalyptus branch were two slugs. Brown with black splotches. They dangled off the brittle branch from their own mucous, coiling around each other like two wet eels. Out of their ends protruded long, bluish-white tendrils that corkscrewed together. The slugs were the length of my hand, or even my arm, glinting in moonlight. Foaming, frothing, fucking. When the branch snapped, the slugs fell splat on the ground. Writhing around. Nibbling at each other. Pooling in their own alien sod and slime. I dry-heaved and deleted the app with the intention of never using it again.

THE TYRES CRUNCHED on loose gravel as I parked my car two doors away from the sickly shell of a house P lived in. It was slapped together with plastic cladding. An architecture for disposability, a thing to be thrown away after use. A few of the people here had homes like this – plastic toy houses – but P's house was punctuated by a single dying tree that looked like a large stick in the dirt. His suburb seemed to declare its own insignificance. It would be a terrible place to start a family.

I messaged him. *I'm waiting outside.* And it dawned on me: after tonight, I'd never see P again.

I was cleaning up the fast-food bags in the car when I heard the shuffle of footsteps on concrete. He wore a black hoodie and sweatpants, though it wasn't very cold. It was perfect. He kept his hands in his pockets; his slender frame was lost in the fabric. Others had been meek, laying their gaze to the ground. But not P. There was a focus in his dark eyes. He never had the prettiest face – his nose was unfit, a little hefty to the sides, wan feminine lips the colour of raisin – but he challenged you, looking you right in the eyes.

When he got in the car beside me, I needed to relax; I took a short breath in, trying to suppress the gut-punch feeling building inside me. I began the drive to our place without a word.

'Damn, you're not cold?' P pretended to warm himself, rustling his hoodie with his hands. His English was proper. Just a whisker away from articulate if it weren't for his slurring.

'No, I am not,' I said.

He poked my bare bicep, which used to be bigger, leaner. 'Showing off those arm muscles?' he asked. That playfulness of his. His kindness out of nowhere. He'd learnt how to get a laugh out of me, and he would have, again, if it weren't for the force increasing in my belly.

'What's wrong…?'

'I can't see you anymore,' I said. 'This will be our last time.'

'No way,' P said. 'What are the chances? I was gonna to tell you the same thing. Or something similar.'

'What?'

'Yep. I found a cute guy my age I like – like, I mean, I'm not cheating on him. We aren't *official* official. But…yeah.' I caught P smiling at this thought, his dimple revealing itself.

'Oh, wow… Congratulations. That's a big thing for you,' I said.

'I was gonna tell you *after* we fucked, though.' P rolled his eyes. 'Way to kill a vibe.'

A thuggish car sped out in front of us, spewing bitter fumes.

'So, are you telling me you were going to do it with me, knowing *that*, and without telling me? That's…a little harsh,' I said.

'Harsh?' P asked.

There it was. The quick-to-move-on-ness. The indifference of his generation.

'You don't feel a little sad?' I asked.

He scoffed, before clearing his throat. 'Sorry. So much to unpack there... No, I don't feel sad.' He looked out the car window while he spoke. 'But I'm glad we met. I'm glad we're going to fuck one last time. Let's make it a good one, yeah? For the whole park to hear.'

'Please do not joke about that. Just enough for us to hear, thank you,' I said.

'And thank you, I guess...for listening to me yap all those times,' he said.

'How do you mean?' I asked.

'You know, like, we didn't really know each other, but I could say whatever. Just vent to you about the whole finding-a-job thing, the coming out, uni, the boy problems –'

'The loneliness,' I said.

'Y-yeah,' he said. 'That too.'

I gave him a tight-lipped smile. I imagined this was what it was like to have patience for a child.

'But I don't know a single thing about you,' he said. 'Not even your name.'

'And you know to leave well enough alone.'

'You married?'

I parked alongside the kerb, ignoring him.

He shrugged his shoulders. 'I guess it's hotter either way.'

I stepped out of my car and scanned the park area. The air was fresh. A single bird, or bat, flew out from the trees to some dark corner of the night. Huddled side by side, P and I walked to our spot in the dark – a bench hidden in the thick of heavy bushes. It seemed to me there was not a single human being awake at this time. Silence pressed down on everything. There were no animals. No bugs. Not a soul. Only the night sky now, framed by the canopy above. Black, a little bluish. Everything touched by the grey glow of moonlight. A lone star glinted from far away. It was as if the park had been cleared out just for us.

'The last time...' I began without thinking.

He didn't hear me – or chose not to – as he threw his hoodie onto the ground. His pure unblemished skin was silken around his slender shape.

He seemed to emanate his own afterglow in the moonlight. He dropped his sweatpants and flipped out his purplish pearl of a penis before standing, wide-legged, and jerking himself to a length I'd never considered before. Even though he'd only wanted to be my hole, nothing but a hole, he looked at me now as if he suddenly wanted everything.

A part of me loosened.

I threw off my clothes and drew him into me, kissing him. He kissed me back. He rooted his tongue down my throat. The taste of him was not at all sour but something else, imitable. He tasted green. Algal. It plunged me into marsh and mire and right at the precipice of retching, I found an overture towards heaven – the spuming in my mouth. He stood on his tiptoes. My back ached a little, and I leant forward a few degrees. P dug his hand inside my underwear. For the first time in my life, my arse was clasped from behind. His hand was cold, but it opened a new world of feeling I didn't think was possible in me. As he held my arse even tighter in his fine hand, my cock ached in unfamiliar ways. A weak groan escaped me. How depraved. How deprived I was. He attempted to push me to the ground, and I, much bigger, flinched only a little. To help him along, I pretended to tumble onto the ragged grass, bracing with my hands before landing on my arse. The last time I'd sat on grass like this must've been when I was young – when time itself stretched infinitely – rolling down hills.

A cold wind cut through the thickets and right through me. P and I considered each other for a second, confused about *what now*, until he started to fiddle with my arms and grapple with my legs, struggling with his angular limbs to turn me onto my hands and knees. It was taking too long for what it was. While he pulled me in baffling directions, I got on all fours for him.

'G-good boy,' he said.

I was almost double his age; I let out a little laugh at this realisation. This was what happened when a group of people gained consciousness and behaviour through screens rather than sincere experience. He drew back his hand to the sky. Paused for a time so sweet and brought it thundering down onto my rear. I whined. An animal's approval.

'Call me a name,' I said.

'Yeah? You want me to call you a name?'

'Yes, yes, do it.'

'Y-you're an ugly fucking bastard!'

Bastard?

'What? No. Do it better. Say something else.'

He pulled on my hair, took in all the air with his lungs and spat in my face. 'Bald-headed bitch!'

I pushed away, wiping off the spit. I was not bald. Maybe thinning a bit, but not *bald*.

'No more names,' I said. 'Just shut up. Just shut the fuck up and hit me harder.'

'Alright.' He gathered himself, straightening his back. 'You ready?'

'Yes. Yes. I am ready,' I said. Unsure of what I was getting ready for. Something good. Something inexplicable. Something only now and never again. It was the fire of the final time.

TRACING MY SKIN, P walked behind, his shadow gathering over me, towering and tall. We'd never reversed roles before. I wondered where he'd learnt all this, if he'd practised with his new guy friend, or if it came with his maturing confidence. Then he kicked my arse with his worn sneakers, clipping my balls. I shrieked out with raw panic. I couldn't draw breath. I fell forward on the ground, squirming.

He was saying something. But my ears were ringing. There was fumbling around my body, a hand on the small of my back to comfort me. Remorse. It hurt him too. Before I could open my mouth, he pulled down my underwear and stuck the tip of his fingernail into the opening of my anus. It forced out of me a shameful noise – the noise of a startled piggy. *Piggy*. I thought of that horrid word now. It was a name my bullies called me. *Useless fat pig.* A name my father called me. *Worthless faggot*. Two of the dirtiest words I'd ever spat at another soul had now charged me with its staggering power. He wiggled the tip of his finger, the pain scratching and swelling at my sphincter. It was then that the universe spun. Stars blurred into trees. Trees blurred into plant litter. I drove my head deep into the ground, soiling my face, wrenching with need, as he pushed the full length of his forefinger inside me. The pointed throbbing spiralled out to a smouldering pleasure. I wanted to be undone, to ride this current of feeling. I was a stunt queen, a devil on the stage. *The only one*. I bit my bottom lip, moaning hard.

'Oh, you sick fuck, you like that? You like that, huh?'

'More,' I said, panting, catching up, catching a single breath. 'More!'

I was everything and nothing but a hole. A trash bin aching to be filled. He hit the bundle of nerves at the base of me with his finger, my penis growing harder, his digit faster and faster.

I came with no hands. A neat, milky line crossed over a twig. A glint of my own mystery. A feeling like spilling a glass of water. Too much of a sudden mess. A surprise – as much to myself as for him. He came thereafter, sputtering, whimpering.

Rain began to fall. Dense bushlands darkened in colour.

I needed to go away. To disappear.

We dressed, flapping off the leaf-fall stuck to our clothes. Treading away through damp bushes, I rushed off in the direction of the car. He followed.

As rain spat from the sky, I smoothed down my hair. Soil covered my hands, knees, cheeks.

Clean. I wanted all of me to be expunged into complete cleanliness.

I wanted to be done. To scrub and bathe until I smelt of nothing.

Not the sex.

Not a father-to-be.

Not myself.

WE DROVE BACK. Only when he pecked my cheek outside his place did I realise I'd been the one steering. His kiss was too much, much too much – foul. It was impossible not to show it on my face. He must have seen it. He looked at me with concern in his eyes.

'You right?' P asked.

The windscreen-wiper blade scraped rain side to side.

'Yes. I'm fine,' I said.

'Cool,' he said. He pulled out his phone, rapid-typed something into the harsh light of the screen before locking it, putting it away, 'Well, that's good.' He gestured to the large container he called a home. 'I'm gonna head now.'

I gave him a nod. He opened the car door, stepped out in the rain and walked off into the gathering dawn.

How long I waited, I had no idea. Time contracted into a headache that hammered from the root of my brain until the first day of December, when Anastasija was born. I drove us back from the hospital that night. I was sick. Something was out of order. The half-empty street had been razed for new developments; the monstrous black sky above was moonless. To my left was the wife, bone-tired and lucent with her postnatal dew. And restrained behind me in the backseat was the little one, bubblegum pink like a piglet and wailing. *Love you*. The words came to me as automatic as turning the roundabout. *I love you*.

Victor Guan Yi Zhou is a writer who grew up on Dharug land. He is currently developing a novel manuscript, which was awarded a 2026 Varuna Residential Fellowship. Victor's short story 'One day, under my Troye Sivan Banksia' was published in the Sweatshop anthology *Povo* (2024), edited by Adam Novaldy Anderson.

NON-FICTION

Operator, please

Notes from an involuntary volunteer

Natalie Kon-yu

OVER THE LAST few years, I've started to do volunteer work for a number of national and international companies. It started off quite slowly. I'm a mother of two young kids and I have a full-time job, so spare time is not something I've got a lot of. But lately the work has picked up.

I don't really like this volunteer work because I always do it in business hours or after school pick-ups, the times when I'm busiest. But I'm lucky to have a full-time job that has semi-flexible hours so that when my volunteer work intrudes upon my working hours, I can just work longer. I'm fortunate that way.

In the last couple of weeks, I've added two more companies to the list. I didn't intend to, and if I'd been told all the terms and conditions from the outset, I would have said, 'No, thank you.' If there's a formal recruitment practice, I haven't encountered it. But here we are.

One is a large electronics manufacturer, with over a hundred billion dollars in revenue and a workforce of who-knows-how-many-millions of people. I should add that the workforce is made up of people who get paid, as well as people like me, who are working for free. The other company I started volunteering at is an Australian company that also earns a huge profit each year. Again, same deal: some paid employees, but a labour force made up mostly of volunteers.

There are so many companies like this – for example, the big department store I gave an hour's work to earlier this year. None of my paid co-workers were rostered on to the luggage department that day, and none of the other paid workers knew enough about luggage to help me. It was a Sunday, and I was told that the luggage person wasn't usually rostered to work weekends. Too expensive, I imagine. So, I got to work. I sat myself down in the corner of the luggage department and spent some time on the internet, trying to find the best kind of suitcases for my work trip. My whole family was there, so my husband tried to keep the kids entertained while I did comparisons of all the luggage this shop offered. Another volunteer turned up, also looking for luggage, so I was able to share the information I found with her. Many hands, as the saying goes, make light work.

In the last fortnight, other volunteer work has consisted of going into a store to do a product comparison, spending forty minutes on hold to another store, finding two head office numbers and sharing them with fellow volunteers, spending twenty minutes waiting for a chatbot to answer me, spending ten minutes crafting a finely worded email only to be given the same wrong answer twice by a chatbot masquerading as a human (which I responded to for fear I'd be kicked out of the system and have to start all over again), keeping a log of a previous phonecall and supplying the new person on the end of the line with the notes I'd kept of my earlier phone meeting so they could update their notes. In the end, I also wound up negotiating with the service company they employed so my concerns could (now) be raised in a timely manner.

That's not all. I've performed peer reviews on my paid colleagues, and I've also provided feedback on the systems my bosses use. I've provided ratings on the products I've bought or the services I've accessed. I've had to stay home at certain times and face responses from my co-workers when I point out I actually have a paying job and that, really, it does come first. I've also had to assemble furniture myself (which is not part of my skill set, I should add). For years, I did it for a big European company that keeps its overheads low, and now I voluntarily do this for any furniture maker I shop from, no matter how pricey.

It's hard to remain temperate when you're working for free. I'm sure I'm not the only one who's had to watch my tone when trying to get their paid co-workers to offer more help. I'm constantly reminded, by an automated recording, that I need to speak nicely to these workers, that rudeness will not be tolerated. And sometimes, after hours of chatbots and fake emails and even more chatbots, I'm tired. I sound curt and annoyed. This often happens when I can see my paid work hours stretching on through dinner time, or when my kids are asking for my help or attention, but I don't want to hang up the phone lest I lose the only human I've encountered who might be able to help me. So, I always make sure I apologise to my paid co-workers. I tell them it's not their fault. I'm not angry at them; I'm angry at our employer, who does not have enough paid employees in furniture showrooms, department stores or customer care to support them. I would like the employer to stop asking so very much of us both.

I DON'T REMEMBER when I started this volunteer work. It could have been ten or fifteen years ago, when I scanned my first trolleyful of shopping at my local supermarket. It was novel at first, sliding the barcodes over the scanner, hearing the satisfying beep. I was young, then, before kids and a full-time job. I didn't mind. But since then, there have been times when my children have grown cranky when I've done this work, and I've found it hard to juggle a toddler on my hip and find the code for bananas. I look for paid co-workers at these times, but they're usually busy helping some other poor volunteer. And I feel for them, too, because there isn't enough of them to go around.

I realise that I'm luckier than lots of my co-volunteers. I'm familiar with computers. I know how to look things up on the internet. Unlike some other volunteers, I don't do shift work, I'm not elderly, and I'm not doing hours and hours of care work every day. Still, I'd like to quit my volunteer jobs. All of them. They do not, as they say, spark joy. In fact, they make me tired and irritable. I just want them to stop.

OF COURSE, I'M being tongue in cheek with my casting of all this activity as volunteering, perhaps to give myself a measure of control over a situation that seems to be getting out of hand. But more and more, these interactions with companies feel like unpaid labour, something I don't think we should have to be doing. If my mattress feels completely different from the one I tested in the store, I don't know why that's my problem to solve. If my washing machine becomes faulty and the small company that the large multi-national company uses to fix it doesn't actually fix it, why do I have to spend hours of my life going back and forth between the two? If my phone company refuses to recognise that their automated system put down the wrong address for us – even if we have screenshots to prove it was not our mistake – why do I have to make call after call trying to get them to resolve a problem not of my own making?

I know I'm not the only one who's had to devote hours of their precious time to getting companies to fix mistakes and to refund or exchange faulty products. According to the 2023 Australian Consumer Survey, '61% of consumers have experienced at least one problem when purchasing a product or service over the past two years.'

A 2024 website post from CHOICE confirms this trend: 'In a survey of over 6,000 CHOICE supporters in May this year, 73% told us they had encountered sub-par service from a business in the preceding year, and 85% believed this assistance was getting worse.'

These numbers seem to indicate the growing distance that corporations are placing between themselves and their customers. If the invention of the call centre in the mid-twentieth century helped this phenomenon along, then the creation of AI chatbots has only accelerated the issue in an alarming way.

An article in *The Guardian* tells us this is not a uniquely Australian problem. Anna Tims writes that 'a report by the thinktank New Britain last month found that 78% of people across the country feel frustrated when dealing with customer services'. Her articles on consumer problems feature horrendous stories of corporate neglect. From disabled pensioners being stranded in foreign countries without their medication to banks erroneously closing customer accounts and energy companies failing to turn on a customer's gas, leaving her family to shiver through a British winter, there's no shortage of horror stories.

But what makes these stories so bad is the underlying issue of corporate neglect. Staff forgetting to wheel a disabled woman onto a plane is bad enough, but the fact that the provider refused to refund the customer the price of the missed flight is another level of shoddy service. The mistake is easy enough to make. Refusing to do anything about it is something else entirely. In fact, the refusal to take responsibility or offer care and assistance is very, very deliberate.

Writing for *The Atlantic*, Chris Colin recently detailed the terrifying story of having a newly purchased car stop working mid-drive. His steering wheel locked up, and his brakes failed to work. After getting out of the car, and having it towed to a mechanic, he suffered a 108-day ordeal of trying to get the car fixed or returned. Colin endured what many of us endure in these situations – dropped calls, unanswered emails, scheduled callbacks that never materialise. He recalls having to tell the same story over and over again to whoever happened to pick up his calls. In researching similar experiences, he also came across the concept of 'sludge', originally articulated by legal scholar Cass R Sunstein. Colin categorises sludge as 'tortuous administrative demands, endless wait times, and excessive procedural fuss that impede us in our lives'.

What Colin discovered is that sludge is not accidental; it's curated and created to stop customers getting satisfactory outcomes for issues with products and providers. He interviewed Amas Tenumah, author of the book *Waiting for Service: An Insider's Account of Why Customer Service Is Broken + Tips to Avoid Bad Service* (2021), who confirmed that a lack of customer care is incentivised by management. Call-centre workers might be told to keep calls under a certain number of minutes; they'll be rewarded for not passing calls up to their supervisors or for keeping to claims targets. In short, they're directed to add roadblocks to the process to protect company profits.

Reading about these instances, and the policies that inform them, is rage-inducing. As I was trawling through the academic literature on chatbots in customer care, it seemed that article after article had been published to help corporations use chatbots in ways that customers find less infuriating – using emojis, apparently, makes us feel more warmly towards these interactions. One recent article, in the *Journal of Service Theory and Practice*, detailed how 'analysing customers' relational, cognitive, affective and behavioural reactions' could guide managers on 'how to develop strategies for handling positive and negative effects' in customer experiences. Here we see that negative encounters are not a problem to be solved in and of themselves. Instead, they're fodder for whatever iteration of 'customer service' might come our way next.

In Australia, it seems we're feeling this lack of concern. The 2023 Australian Consumer Survey also states that 40 per cent of respondents sense that businesses don't care, and 34 per cent said businesses refused to accept fault. The issue of sludge is also relevant, with 16 per cent of respondents saying 'they could not get hold of the business or manufacturer after finding the issue'. All of these numbers had increased since the 2016 survey, but the last one had tripled in that time.

What's worrying is that these practices are having a profound effect – not on businesses but on consumers. There's been a 10 per cent drop in consumers taking action to resolve their issues because of 'the perception that it will take a lot of effort'. The report also shows that fewer than half of customers are satisfied with their resolutions. One wonders if these numbers are based only on the outcome, or if they also take into consideration the gruelling journey that consumers undertake to resolve an issue. As CHOICE reports, 'large numbers of Australians are experiencing poor customer service and many of us feel the standard of support provided by businesses is getting worse.'

In the face of poor customer service and ever-increasing amounts of sludge poured between us and the solution, many people are simply not prepared to try to get their issues fixed at all, preferring to put up with faulty products or replace them themselves, all of which helps no one but the companies.

We can guess why this issue is now so pervasive. Writing in 2019, Anthony Dukes and Yi Zhu posited that terrible customer experiences continue to proliferate because it's profitable for the companies who engage in them. As time goes on, we're seeing the propagation of huge companies, which results in a lack of choice in the market for consumers. When you have just a couple of supermarkets to shop from, you're more likely to shop at the one that treats you less shittily. The shift in language from 'customer' to 'consumer' doesn't help much either – more and more, we're seen less as people and increasingly as individual markets to capture. Colin posits that part of the issue is the way CEO tenures have become shorter; for this reason, they prioritise returns to shareholders and investors over building their customer base. Tims concurs, stating that the companies who rank most highly in the UK Customer Satisfaction Index are not owned by shareholders. She writes: 'When shareholder dividends are not the primary focus, investment can prioritise customer care over quick profits.'

Tims also points out that in the UK, people spend 'between 28 and 41 minutes every week dealing with (companies) in lengthy battles'. And these numbers are based only on those willing to put in the work.

ALL THIS BRINGS us back to the fact that wading through this sludge is a form of labour – one that's not being remunerated. Moreover, it's time wrested away from the other things we have to do: paid labour and care work. If someone bothered to ask us if we'd be willing to donate between twenty-eight and forty-one minutes to help create profits for investors and shareholders, our answer, quite naturally, would likely be an emphatic *no*.

I've always envisaged volunteering at some point in my life, when I'm no longer working full time and the kids are old enough to need me less urgently. I'd like to volunteer for organisations that help integrate refugees. Or teach creative writing to people who can't afford to pay for classes. I could volunteer to a helpline or cook meals for people who need them. This is the kind of volunteer work I think would actually matter to my community, the kind of work that could do the most good.

By contrast, volunteering for these corporations does not feel like giving back to my community. I don't think I'm making the world a kinder place by measuring my mattress or scanning groceries. I don't think my community is being well served by my feedback on products and services. And I worry about a great fatigue settling over all of us when we do so much volunteer work for these profit-hungry corporations. I'd like to call someone and complain, but I haven't yet found their number.

Natalie Kon-yu is a writer and academic. She is the author of critically acclaimed *The Cost of Labour: How Women Are Trapped by the Politics of Pregnancy and Parenting*, which was named in the Australia Institute's reading list for 2022. She is also a co-commissioning editor of *#MeToo: Stories from the Australian Movement* (Affirm Press, 2019), *Mothers and Others* (Macmillan, 2015) and *Just Between Us* (Macmillan, 2013).

NON-FICTION

Gold standard

The conscious uncoupling of banking and democracy

Hannah Forsyth

NOT LONG AFTER the 2018 Royal Commission into Misconduct in the Banking, Superannuation and Financial Services Industry, I attended a panel discussion that sought to consider its professional and ethical implications for bankers. Anna Bligh, CEO of the Australian Banking Association at the time, persistently used the #notallbankers hashtag, which was stretched beyond all rational use during the commission. Despite a #fewbadapples, she suggested, bank integrity was secure: Australians could sleep well at night knowing their money was safe.

Until then, it had never occurred to me that my money – such as it is – might *not* be safe in the bank. These institutions go to some trouble to present themselves as symbols of safety, stability and trustworthiness. For example, there was great excitement when the Commonwealth Bank's vault – still one of the largest in the world – was hauled to Sydney's Martin Place in 1926 by the twenty-five horses required to transport it. It was a public spectacle that demanded our trust in banking, saying *look at the hefty measures the bank takes to protect your money*. Banks are now more likely to flaunt their investment in cybersecurity, scam prevention and online fraud, like the ANZ Falcon® technology that 'works around the clock' in a way that's 'personal to each and every one of our customers'. The message is the same: sure, we have big bucks, but we use them to keep your money safe.

These days, although banks do much more than store cash, we have no choice but to use them for that core purpose. Back in 1990, when I had my first job, I received a little orange pay packet containing $14.75 – but wages are now deposited directly into the bank, so most of us cannot have a job without a bank account. With less cash circulating since Covid, we now literally tap our bank deposits when we buy stuff. Today, almost every transaction in our economy is managed (also overseen and sold as aggregated data) by banks.

As these institutions have grown more powerful, Australians have understandably become wary. The fact that banks function independently of any democratic process is an anomaly in our political system. It's a historical curiosity that begins with the connection between everyday Australian banking and mid-nineteenth-century gold fever.

DURING THE 1850s gold rush, a person who struck gold found their elation quickly supplanted by anxiety. Where would they keep it? How would they protect it? In this environment, banks offered the only real answer – and soon enough, they grew like mad.

At that time, banks mainly served merchants. An Australian wool merchant, for example, might have a contract to sell wool in London but need cash to pay for the cost of getting it there. The bank would lend the merchant the amount of the contract up-front, but with a 'discount' – so that when the merchant repaid the bank at the conclusion of the deal, the bank made a profit. This model of banking was so ingrained that before the gold rush, some Australian banks didn't even take deposits. It wasn't so much that ordinary people didn't have bank accounts – they just weren't the bank's business. That was about to change.

For most of the people converging on the new gold-rush towns in Victoria and New South Wales, making a gold deposit was their first encounter with banking. The gold rush turned everyday banking into a reverse sort of alchemy, converting gold into money. George Preshaw, a gold-rush banker, described a digger who listened carefully about the nature of the deposit he was making, completed the transaction and stepped outside the bank. A moment later, he stepped back in and withdrew the money, holding the cash he'd received like it was some sort of miracle.

And it was. Ore from the ground was converted into a bank deposit. That abstract thing, the deposit, represented money that really belonged to him.

Finding a place to safely keep the gold – or, rather, to sell the gold, converting mining into deposits that in turn became currency – arguably marked the beginning of typical modern banking in Australia. Before long, banks were central to the entire economy. The entanglement of banking with the rise of industrial waged labour was what turned the former from a marginal industry on the edges of international shipping into the indispensable piece of economic infrastructure it is now.

But as their lives became ever more entangled with banks, members of the working class started to smell a rat. A newspaper story from 1906 captured the vibe, portraying an imaginary banker speaking to a fictional Irish bartender called Mr Dooley:

> Ye sleep better at nights because ye feel that ye'er money is where no wan can reach it except over me dead body. If ye on'y knew ye'd not turned ye-er back before I chased those hard-earned dollars off the premises. With yer money I build a house an' rent it to you. I start a railroad with it, an' ye wurruk on th' railroad at two dollars a day.

This was a fair assessment: most bank customers were capitalist enterprisers and property investors who relied on working-class labour, rent and consumption. But the banks were also becoming powerful because of the expansion of modern government.

The democratic institutions that workers helped build also needed banks, boosting their spectacular growth. Government debt – which frequently takes the form of bonds – has been central to the operation of parliaments for hundreds of years. In the Australian colonies, an alliance between banking and government was modelled on the Bank of England: banks supplied the cash needed for everyday governing, protected government tax income and, crucially, sold government bonds to fund public spending.

As governments grew in the Australian colonies, their debt tied the state to the world's finance centre, the City of London, which was the only place (until the rise of New York) with sufficient resources for such big loans. The London banks enjoyed their power over Australian governments, using their status to wield influence. In 1921, for example, they put a black ban on loans to the government of Queensland, hoping to push Labor out of office by cutting off their credit supply. In 1930, at the height of the Great Depression, the Australian Government endured a humiliating visit by British banker Sir Otto Niemeyer, who informed the government that because the City held its debt, the City would also be determining government fiscal policy.

The Niemeyer episode is famous in Australian history, primarily for the immediate political fallout involving New South Wales Premier Jack Lang, who refused to comply with Niemeyer's plan, and the compromise (the left saw it as a sellout) enabled by what became known as the Premiers' Plan (which sought 'equality of sacrifice' between capital and labour by cutting spending *and* bond payments).

Obsessed as we are with politicians, we tend to overlook the role banks have played, and continue to play, in our political system. Just as we see the legal system as the third arm of executive government, so we might see banking as the fourth.

Dooley's fictional 1906 banker had something to say about this, too:

> Ye'er money makes me a prominent citizen. Th' newspapers interview me on what shud be done with th' toilin' masses, meaning ye an' Donohue; I construcht the foreign policy iv th' Government; I tell ye how ye shud vote. Ye've got to vote the way I say or I won't give ye back ye'er money.

Perhaps the banking sector has long had good reason to conceal its centrality to Australia's democratic and economic management.

IN THE EARLY 1990s, Treasurer Paul Keating introduced compulsory superannuation, launching a new phase in the connection between politics and finance. Who controls this money is subject to continual political conflict; in 2018, Liberal Party politicians vainly hoped the Royal Commission would expose corruption in industry funds whose boards include union representatives. As it turned out, it wasn't the unions that were the problem. It was the banks.

Over the last few decades, the pool of Australian savings has grown to more than $4 trillion, approximately the global domestic product of Hong Kong. Except for worker representation on the boards of industry funds, it's almost the sole plaything of the finance industry. Our finance sector is proud of this pot of money, which is the second or third largest globally. Our superannuation savings make Australian finance even more influential than Dooley's banker claimed, because with our money they are one of the biggest investors in the world.

They better have a damned good vault.

They don't. After the Royal Commission, journalist Michael Roddan was scathing: 'The banking sector had been covering up the big Australian rort,' he wrote in *The People vs the Banks* (2019). 'In its world, superannuation members came dead last. It was other people's money, but the fund managers saw it as theirs for the taking.' Indeed, the 'big four banks and AMP were far and away some of the worst handlers of Australia's savings'.

The story of Australia's massive superannuation pot is further important, however, because it represents a major shift in our democracy since the 1990s.

Compulsory superannuation sought to reduce the burden of the aged pension on the federal budget. Taking care of our elderly citizens was previously a government responsibility, but it is now largely the task of banks. This set-up offers distinctive advantages to the wealthy and has systematically disadvantaged women in ways that the aged pension never could.

Having outsourced superannuation, the Australian Government remained anxious about the pensions they'd have to pay, particularly as the population on average had become older, lowering the relative proportion of people in the workforce. In 2004, Treasurer Peter Costello announced a sovereign wealth fund, the so-called Future Fund. This sort of thing was more common for countries like China, Kuwait and Russia than OECD democracies such as Australia – in fact, the billions these sovereign wealth funds controlled were cause for concern among democratic nations, who feared such a large quantity of foreign investment could be used politically, undermining democratic sovereignty.

But once Costello handed billions of government funding to the finance sector to grow wealth for the state's pension liability, other transfers of governmental responsibility to finance grew further still. Now, the Future Fund also looks after disability support, medical research, disaster preparedness and relief (including droughts), social and affordable housing, and the Indigenous Land and Sea Corporation, which supports First Nations economic opportunity. In March 2025, the Future Fund was valued at $307.6 billion, which is around thirty times the Commonwealth Bank's 2025 profit.

This is money that the government chooses not to redistribute in the present but saves for the future.

An ominously titled Board of Guardians and a selected handful of investment managers – 114, according to the website – invest *some* of that money in real-world infrastructure and real estate, but the rest is in a diversified set of financial stuff circulating in stock markets in Australia and overseas, as well as a bunch of credit, including home loans. Some is held in cash, which includes US Treasury Bonds. That means that on top of the $4 trillion or so of our personal superannuation, around $300 billion of our collective wealth, embodying the government's capacity to do some of its most essential work, is circulating through the global finance sector.

What could go wrong?

THIS OUTSOURCING OF government responsibility to the finance sector reversed the findings of an earlier banking royal commission, established by Joseph Lyons' United Australia Party government and conducted over 1936 and 1937. Global finance was implicated in the Great Depression, demonstrating that perhaps our money might not be safe with the banks – which is why the public demanded a royal commission in the first place. This episode culminated a decade later in a major political battle that the banks won, setting us on the path to a finance sector that governs much of our lives – including the security of our retirement.

Among the commission's conclusions was a boring recommendation for regular collection of banking statistics. It's typical of public servants to seek ever more data, perhaps. But in this case, it was also crucial to the task of monitoring bank profits, which the commissioners asked of government. The purpose was to ensure that trading banks were keeping money circulating in the economy, without which, the report said, 'no branch of industry' could carry on under 'modern industrial conditions'. If their profits, which would now be disclosed, exceeded the 'fair return for the services rendered', the commissioners suggested, 'the Government should consider whether the profits of the trading banks should be regulated or limited as in the case of some public utilities'.

The final report of the Royal Commission on Monetary & Banking Systems in Australia included a dissenting view prepared by future Prime

Minister Ben Chifley, who was one of the six commissioners alongside a Supreme Court judge, an accountant, an economist and a stockbroker who was also a leading member of the Country Party. Chifley wanted to go much further than the other commissioners by actively limiting bank profits. 'Banking differs from any other form of business because any action – good or bad – by a banking system affects almost every phase of national life,' he wrote. For Chifley, that meant the banks' only aim should be the 'general good of the community'. Just after unemployment hit 13.1 per cent in 1929, Chifley said, the banks raised interest rates. For those with wealth, the rate hike meant their earnings were joyfully increased, but for anyone with a loan – well, 'This action of the banks, in my opinion, was quite wrong as far as the community was concerned,' Chifley argued, 'although it did bring some immediate additional profits to the banks.'

The 1937 commissioners all agreed that banks were akin to a public utility. We might debate appropriate parallel utilities, but I quite like sewerage. The sewerage system is essential. Like the economy, it has flows and circulations, and its regulation is a lynchpin of community wellbeing, indeed our collective health.

Also, obviously, it's full of shit.

Unlike our 2018 commissioners, who observed (bull)shit throughout the system, Chifley was not accusing the banks of any dishonesty. He simply thought it was impossible for the banks to focus on the community while there was a profit motive. In the absence of nationalisation, which he preferred, Chifley suggested a systemic limit on profits at 'an amount equal to 5 per cent of shareholders' funds, or 8 per cent per annum on paid capital, whichever is less'.

A decade later, as prime minister presiding over postwar reconstruction, Chifley decided to nationalise the banks. This was a longstanding Labor policy, yet everyone was surprised, not least because of the 'rash' way he proclaimed bank nationalisation: in a forty-two-word announcement on a Saturday morning, heard by a tiny handful of diehard journalists who might have been skiving off from taking the kids to sport.

To Chifley, the banks were still a public utility, and that reason alone would have motivated nationalisation. However, they were also essential to postwar reconstruction, providing the finance for the massive expansion of urgently needed housing and underpinning the economic conditions that would enable the government's new full-employment policy.

Chifley said that the two Bank Acts tabled in 1945, one for the Commonwealth Bank and the other for the trading banks, would enable government to 'accept responsibility for the economic condition of the nation'. He was in the middle of postwar reconstruction, where economic reorganisation was 'of such magnitude and involve[d] such serious consequences that no other attitude could be maintained'.

Neither Act set out to nationalise the banks. Chifley's Cabinet decided on that when the banks, led by the CEO of what's now the National Australia Bank (NAB), disputed the Act. The High Court concurred that requiring local governments to hold deposit accounts with the Commonwealth Bank, a cashflow that would help with the government's housing plans, was unconstitutional. But Chifley and his cabinet agreed that without the new Act, they wouldn't be able to take responsibility for the 'economy of the nation'. It's tough maintaining public health when you can't control the flow of sewage.

A spoiler alert at this point is hardly needed: bank nationalisation failed.

Much of that was due to the CEO of NAB, Sir Leslie McConnan, who in 1945 was only just getting warmed up. I hear there's a portrait of McConnan in Melbourne's NAB museum as the hero who 'saved the banks'.

Let's be clear: the banks were not being 'destroyed'. The plan was compulsory acquisition in the national interest. The government proposed to purchase them at an independently calculated fair price. Shareholders would be reimbursed. And every single bank worker would keep their job, at the same pay rate. Indeed, banks would operate as they had been. But all Australians, not just a handful of shareholders, would now be the beneficiaries of their service and the profits they produced – presumably also without the bad behaviour those profits coerced, and that became so obvious in the 2018 Royal Commission.

By 1947, a massive, co-ordinated public relations campaign was launched by the banks, led by McConnan and exploited by then Opposition Leader Robert Menzies. Bank customers, newspapers and crowded events were bombarded with propaganda about 'saving' the banks from what they called an authoritarian communist government. The anti-nationalisation agenda was so noisy that when Chifley lost the 1949 election, many people said (and still say) it was because of his stance on banking. And maybe it was. But Chifley had not only alienated anti-communists over the banking issue; he'd also pissed off the left in 1949 when he arrested union leaders, froze union funds and sent in the military to break a coalmine strike. There were not enough voters in the middle allow Chifley to win.

THAT 1949 ELECTION still shapes the question of who controls the money. To think about this question, we need to look at central banking.

The initial idea, articulated as early as 1824, was that if the government owned the bank, they would not need to pay interest on their £15 million loan from the Bank of England. Rather than remain a distant customer of the Bank of England, the Australian Government would have its own bank. Other ideas that were developing around the same time about a system of government and a national bank entangled the interests of our democratic institutions with the finance sector.

Since the eighteenth century, the Bank of England had sold government bonds to London folk looking to make money from money, including other bankers. Every day, bankers moved bonds and money around London (on foot), then convened with other bankers at the end of the day for 'clearing'. There, bankers counted what had moved between institutions and settled the leftovers, ready to begin again tomorrow. For a century, before there was any expectation that ordinary people had a bank account, this set of practices, alongside discounting merchant contracts, formed the basis of modern banking.

Because bonds became so important to the whole system, the central bank took on a dual role: performing material operations for government and maintaining the stability of the finance system (which sometimes means acting as a 'lender of last resort' during a crisis; in recent decades, it's become about using interest rates to control inflation). The emergence of this double role produced the key political tension in Australia's banking history, for there can be a significant difference between acting in the national interest and supporting the finance sector's rate of profit.

The first central bank was the Commonwealth Bank, formed in 1911 as an instrument of Australian Federation to serve the Australian Government. It was simultaneously a commercial and central bank, intended to facilitate the movement of money across state borders. The profits flowed back into public coffers, doubly supporting the functions of parliamentary democracy.

But in 1949, emboldened by their success in opposing nationalisation, the trading banks successfully lobbied to separate the Commonwealth Bank's commercial functions from its role as a central bank. HC 'Nugget' Coombs, who had led postwar reconstruction and was by then Governor of the Commonwealth Bank, said separation of trading and central banking simplified relationships with the finance sector. But his pragmatism was tinged with regret that the government-owned trading bank wouldn't any longer supply funds to the government. This was the end of any vision for a banking system that would put the national good first, with profits flowing back into the economy, or enabling the work of government.

At least the central bank maintained its mandate for full employment, which was the lynchpin of Coombs' postwar reconstruction plan.

The central bank was renamed the Reserve Bank of Australia (RBA) in 1960 and kept its dual role as a manager of public debt and as a 'bankers' bank' with responsibility for the finance sector. Within a decade, its responsibility for monetary policy deepened, controlling the flow of money (these days, mostly credit) into society, which further embedded the RBA into the everyday lives of Australians.

Before the 1970s, it was easy. The US dollar, itself stabilised by gold, acted to regulate global currencies. This *was* the monetary policy – in controlling the value of Australian money, the global system also controlled inflation, pretty much. But in 1971, US President Richard Nixon ended dollar–gold convertibility, which undermined the basis for stabilising global currencies. Then Arab oil producers punished the West for supporting Israel by restricting oil supply, causing massive shocks. Both led to 'stagflation', a stagnant economy with a massive inflation problem. Traditional government fiscal tools would not work; they needed active monetary policy.

The RBA's job suddenly became difficult. It was an important job, arguably still the key tool for managing the economy. Fiscal policy, even when it works, tends to have a slower effect.

Conditions favoured 'monetarism', restricting the quantity of money to drive down inflation. This austerity bolstered neoliberal opposition to democracy's tendency to redistribute wealth, believing, without evidence, in democracy's 'natural profligacy'.

When it came to displays of profligacy, however, the banks said, 'Hold my beer.'

One RBA governor described how bank deregulation, which began in the early 1970s and was likely the only plausible response to the change in the role of the US dollar, meant bankers 'were like a bunch of kids set loose for the first time in a lolly shop'. The system was flooded with cheap credit, producing the likes of Alan Bond and Christopher Skase, who accrued unpayable debts – and ultimately ripped off Australians.

In the late 1980s, when, under the Hawke–Keating Accord, wages were suppressed to maintain employment (offset by tax cuts to the lowest earners), the RBA raised interest rates to 18 per cent. It worked, lowering inflation. Soon enough, the RBA saw other forms of wage suppression as its mandate, such as redefining what Chifley and Coombs meant by 'full employment' at the end of the Second World War: they now increase unemployment until inflation stops and then call *that* 'full employment'.

This is purposeful redistribution of the opposite kind to the one that neoliberals thought characterised democratic governments. Rather than governmental 'profligacy' that redistributes income to reduce inequality, this system forces the poor to pay for the cost of anti-inflationary strategy. You see, very high inflation is bad for everyone, but a little can be useful, especially for reducing debt. But inflation is *always* bad for banks. The value of their biggest asset, the loan book, shrinks. When global events cause inflation, the banks want it stopped, fast – but they don't want to pay for it.

The RBA's job as the bankers' bank makes protecting the finance system their priority. Australia's poorest and most vulnerable pay the price.

DESPITE MYRIAD APOLOGIES in 2018, banks do not appear to have changed. In 2024, the Australian Securities and Investments Commission found that banks 'knowingly' ensured millions of customers paid high fees when, as poorer members of the community, they were entitled to lower fees. The Commonwealth Bank says it won't refund them. That bank made a $10.25 billion profit in 2025. The structure observed by Mr Dooley's imaginary banker has prevailed, at least in this case. Banks readily take money, often from the poorest and hardest working Australians. They then try – very, very hard – not to give it back.

This pattern reveals a systemic weakness in our democracy. Private interests have taken control of a public utility. Then the system demands the public pay for its stabilisation by keeping a segment of the population unemployed on below-poverty income, destabilising families and social cohesion. Billions of dollars of bank profit – $15.5 billion *after* tax, last year, just for the Big Four – must come from somewhere.

Banking and democracy grew together, but they have since grown apart. Protecting our democracy, economy and retirement savings requires us to think carefully about how they can be reunited.

Hannah Forsyth is a historian based in the Blue Mountains. She is the author of *Virtue Capitalists: The Rise and Fall of the Professional Class in the Anglophone World* (Cambridge University Press, 2023) and *A History of the Modern Australian University* (NewSouth, 2014). You can follow Hannah's work at hannahforsyth.substack.com.

Troy Wong

Year of the Snake

celebrate the Year of the Snake

with Penfolds! Marshall is marking
this Lunar New Year with a special

edition Emberton III speaker
new skins, old ectotherms
年年 *another flat chinoiserie*
to honour all asian cultures

Allen's are releasing the Allen's
Year of the Snake Lucky Snakes

Alive! in 888g bags rrp $14.44
another tactless repackaging
at our expense
the auspicious red and gold

Dyson Airstrait hair straightener
pays homage to Lunar New Year

as well as Valentine's Day
extraction and exaltation
are an inseparable two-in-one
so step into 2025 with a new pair

of snake-embossed Dr Martens
featuring gold-rimmed eyelets

and lucky red accents
colours without culture
a language clowned for comedy
in the Year of the Wood Snake

the new North Face
Nuptse jacket with snake coil

pattern motif signifies
they will never stop
exploring ways to exploit
the wisdom and the mystery

of ancient traditions   this january
salute all the snakes

you know and love with
Sorbent's limited edition
Lunar New Year
Lotion Tissues   perfect

for saucy snags and any
other spills you might make

this Australia Day

Troy Wong is an Australian poet born to Singaporean parents. His work, written on unceded Dharug and Gadigal land, is published or forthcoming in *Antipodes*, *Australian Poetry Journal*, *Cordite*, *Island*, *Locative*, *The Marrow*, *Palette*, *The Suburban Review* and the anthology *Solid Air* (UQP, 2019). He is a winner of The Nomad Review 'Fragility' Poetry Prize, an Australian Poetry Slam National Finalist, and the founder and creative director of Bread & Butter Poetry Slam.

NON-FICTION

How meme coins explain the world

Understanding the new currency of charisma

Chris Vasantkumar

THE MESSAGE POSTED on the $TRUMP website on 12 May 2025 reads like the opening gambit of an internet scam: 'Congratulations, if you're in the top 220 on the leaderboard we will be contacting you in the next 24 hours. Check your inbox (and spam folder) and expect a phone call for the Trump Official Dinner invitation and details… President Trump will see YOU on May 22 at the Gala Dinner in Washington D.C.' Nonetheless, not even two weeks later, 215-odd men and, according to one attendee, 'five to eight' women trooped louchely into the plush confines of Trump National Golf Club in Sterling, Virginia. The guests were all aficionados of TrumpCoin, the presidential cryptocurrency introduced to duelling fanfares of hagiography and execration in early January 2025. Known, at least initially, only by their crypto wallet addresses, they paid between US$55,000 and $37.7 million for this audience with the President, the cost per plate averaging out to a cool million dollars.

Dinner featured a 'Trump organic field green salad', a choice of filet mignon or pan-seared halibut, with mashed potatoes and cooked vegetables of questionable provenance, followed by warm lava cake. Punters received a souvenir hat and a copy of the 'coin' itself. Oddly, the latter looks nothing like its monetary antecedents, instead taking the form of what *USA Today* described as a 'gaudy baseball card' featuring the words 'FIGHT FIGHT FIGHT' superimposed over the now familiar image of Trump standing with a defiant raised fist after surviving an attempt on his life in Pennsylvania in July 2024. Attendees were also treated/subjected to a roughly twenty-five-minute address by the President in which he pronounced, 'There is a lot of sense in crypto. A lot of common sense in crypto. And we're honoured to be working on helping everybody here.' Afterwards, without any further audience interaction, Trump departed by golf cart to his waiting helicopter, accompanied by the familiar strains of Village People's 'YMCA'.

At least some of the guests were left cold by the whole affair. In an interview with CNBC, twenty-five-year-old entrepreneur/influencer Nick Pinto, who reportedly spent US$500,000 on TrumpCoin to secure what had been billed as 'the most EXCLUSIVE INVITATION in the world', lamented the quality of the food ('it sucked'), the fact that his water glass was filled only once, and the content of Trump's speech ('pretty much bullshit').

Others in attendance included former NBA player Lamar Odom, touting his own personal cryptocurrency, the typographically unfortunate $ODOM (insert $GOMORRAH joke here) as well as TrumpCoin's top holder, billionaire Chinese-born crypto investor Justin Sun, who was returning to the US for the first time since a Biden-era civil fraud lawsuit filed against him by the Securities and Exchange Commission was dropped under controversial circumstances in the aftermath of Trump's second inauguration. While Sun and the twenty-four other biggest investors had been treated to a personal audience with the President and a VIP tour of the White House before the gala, the remaining crypto believers had to be content with simply being in the same room as the man himself.

As Miles Klee wrote in *Rolling Stone*, 'It had to be something of a disappointment for guests, including foreign executives, who went with the idea of swaying Trump on crypto issues and regulation.' Yet for at least some of the guests, this proximity more than sufficed. *ITV News* reported that Kendall Davis – a young, formerly homeless African-American crypto investor – 'credited the industry with making him a multimillionaire', describing 'the event as a rare, once-in-a-lifetime chance to share a meal with a sitting president'.

Critics' responses to Trump's meme-coin dinner were predictably scathing. Sitting Democratic Senator Jeff Merkley, who joined the ranks of protestors lining the route to the golf club, dubbed the gathering the 'Mount Everest of corruption'. Another Democratic senator, Elizabeth Warren, criticised Trump for using the presidency to enrich himself in unprecedented ways. Others highlighted how the sizeable TrumpCoin investments of the participants were, in effect, payments to Trump that sidestepped regulations on both the size of campaign contributions and the involvement of foreign donors in American politics. In response, the White House held that Trump had merely attended the event as a guest himself and hadn't used it as a means of soliciting political contributions.

Other internet users noted with some schadenfreude that 43 per cent of the 220 'winners' had actually lost money – in some cases, a lot of money – on their TrumpCoin punts. According to *The Guardian*, by the time the dinner was held in late May, ninety-five unlucky top investors had incurred a combined net loss of US$8.95 million since the coin's launch five months prior. The same article also noted that such losses align with broader trends: 'It's believed that 764,000 wallets – mostly belonging to small holders – have lost money on $TRUMP, according to data from the cryptocurrency and blockchain analysis firm Chainalysis. Meanwhile, just 58 wallets have made more than US$10m each on their purchases of the coin.'

Such disparities between the profits of a few and the losses of the many are not unique to TrumpCoin but also apply to meme coins more generally. So, given the likelihood of being parted from one's money, what's been driving the ebbs and flows of what one commenter has described as 'crypto's stupidest bubble'? What's the point of a meme coin in the first place?

THE ANSWER TO this question has eluded many critics of crypto (and even some of its advocates). In *Rolling Stone*, Mark Hays dismissed Trump's meme coin as 'one part a vehicle for personal profit, one part a playground taunt over federal ethics rules, and one part a crypto-fascist pledge of allegiance'. In *The New Yorker*, David D Kirkpatrick has highlighted the lack of gravitas of both $TRUMP in particular and meme coins more broadly: '$TRUMP doesn't purport to hold value in the way that bitcoin or stablecoins do,' he writes. 'Nor does $TRUMP entitle a buyer to a vote on a company's future direction, as World Liberty's initial token does. It does not even convey the right to own a digital cartoon of Trump. It's a meme coin, a novelty, a bit of fun – the fun, for those who enjoy it, of paying Donald Trump.' Interviewed in *USA Today*, Andy Baehr, the managing director and head of product at CoinDesk and an advocate for the respectability of the crypto sector, decried TrumpCoin as bad for an industry 'that was trying very hard to demonstrate that it's serious, that it welcomes useful regulation, that it wants to be more regulated'. Trump's high-profile move into meme coins threatens to derail all of this, he bristled, in no small part because meme coins are 'definitionally and unashamedly frivolous' and without 'any utility'.

If crypto is something of a joke in mainstream finance, then meme coins are often seen this way by mainstream crypto's boosters, who often deride them as mere 'shitcoins' – either a sucker's play or a trifle unworthy of serious attention. Yet, for my money, far from being a novelty, the meme coin is crucial to understanding the contemporary moment. Its appeal illuminates some alarming aspects of emergent economic and political practices and sentiments that are intimately connected to the rise of Trumpism in America and the forces of populism, authoritarianism and the right globally.

TO MAKE SENSE of these claims, we first have to understand how meme coins differ from more traditional forms of crypto. Meme coins are cryptocurrencies whose value derives from their users' membership in communities of affect. 'Legitimate' forms of cryptocurrency – bitcoin being the most famous, alongside Ethereum and other 'altcoins' with actual use cases and/or claims to technological innovation – are valued, at least in part, for their usefulness (actual or anticipated) in solving problems to do with the speed, security and/or functionality of peer-to-peer digital transactions. By contrast, meme coins lack use cases beyond their affective appeal – any value they might accrue is based on 'vibes' rather than a rational argument for their uptake. Here, TrumpCoin is actually representative. As Marquette University's David Krause puts it, 'the $TRUMP white paper explicitly acknowledges the token's limited utility, stating its primary role as a community-driven and symbolic asset rather than a functional currency… Emphasi[sing] community engagement, the white paper highlights that the $TRUMP token's value is largely tied to sentiment rather than practical applications.'

From a glass-half-empty perspective, this means that meme coins are indeed essentially frivolous – nothing other than dangerously volatile and in some senses delusionally speculative investments, reliant entirely on sentiment for their valuation. From a less dismissive perspective, however, we can see the value of meme coins as deriving precisely from their capacity to both betoken and cultivate membership in affective communities. For some enthusiasts (such as the pseudonymous author of a Bitget.com explainer), the community is precisely the point: 'In the words of Richard Dawkins,' they write, 'a meme is a "unit of culture." Let's respect that definition and remember why we're in crypto – not just to make money, but to belong.' (Nonetheless we must bear in mind that such communities are not commonly wholesome, inclusive or pleasant, often channelling the worst strains of misogyny, racism and nihilism endemic to the contemporary internet.)

A 2025 *Guardian* piece based on an interview with Professor of Finance Carol Alexander suggests that users buy $TRUMP 'to show their support for the president. In this way, it's similar to a "fan token", like those produced by sports teams and players.' Similarly, Krause notes the collective aspects of TrumpCoin 'as a community-driven asset with limited practical utility… It encourages engagement among Trump supporters and connects them with related initiatives within a blockchain ecosystem.' Moreover, he suggests, 'the token also functions as a digital representation of Trump's brand, appealing to his followers while offering speculative trading opportunities. Similar to owning Green Bay Packer stock, the $TRUMP coin emphasizes participation over practical use, encouraging a sense of belonging to Trump's movement.'

Ironically, perhaps, given the recency of this trend, TrumpCoin as a token of political belonging harks back to the origins of coins themselves in ancient Greece. According to geographer Erica Schoenberger, 'the history of gold coinage in antiquity is rooted in the contest for political power: it runs not from barter to coin but from personal seal to coin.' The first Greek coins 'were very much about exchange but not at all about commodity exchange'; instead, 'discs of gold stamped with the personal seal of the gift giver' figured prominently among the objects involved in the 'lavish gift exchange' used 'to bind [political] leaders and their allies more closely together'. As such, 'precious metal coins in Greece start out as a medium of political exchange and a store of political value.'

What's more, neither Alexander's nor Krause's relatively anodyne take really captures the deeply felt nature of the matrix of belonging that both spawns and is spawned by successful meme coins. Anthropologist William Mazzarella, who has written extensively on the affective dimensions of populism, traces the 'uncanny line' from the symbolic charge of membership in the contemporary Trumpist right to early Christian communities. Drawing on the work of theologian Robert Yelle, he homes in on the Pauline distinction between 'the holy *charism* (God's grace)' and '*nomos* (law – both Roman and Jewish)'. Mazzarella argues that this distinction 'marked and animated the [early] Christian community as a *shared body*, at once physical, spiritual, and political. Every time Trump voters are dismissed as a "basket of deplorables," the attack isn't just symbolic. It's *substantial* – felt as an assault on a shared body. And on the world in which that body wants to live.'

Participation in contemporary charismatic communities of sentiment – political, religious and economic – thus goes 'much deeper than the usual sense in which the word is used in democratic theory to suggest an active involvement in an institutional democratic process'. Instead of calm, measured, civic-minded engagement with the substance of policy and a rational commitment to the democratic process, Mazzarella suggests that 'charismatic participation involves an elated experience of shared bodily substance'. In such a context, TrumpCoin, like the MAGA hat, emerges as a fragment of the sacred, of what Australian political scientist Michael Dutton has termed 'the smallest unit[s] of an affective cosmos'. Understanding both $TRUMP and meme coins more generally therefore requires us to 'consider human motivations that', per Mazzarella, 'may have very little to do with the presumption of rational self-interest with which most economists and some political scientists like to work'.

IN THE CONTEXT of meme coins, a focus on heroic action has gone hand in hand with the emphases on affect and belonging since the beginning. The first meme coin, Dogecoin, was introduced in 2013 as a send-up of bitcoin by two software engineers. Nonetheless, it quickly amassed a substantial community of online supporters that was later famously galvanised into the 'Doge Army' by the mercurial Twitter interventions of Elon Musk between December 2020 and May 2021. This unprecedented support prompted rapid spikes in Dogecoin's valuation – until the bloom began to come off the rose in the aftermath of Musk's infamous appearance on *Saturday Night Live* in which he admitted during a skit that Dogecoin was essentially 'a hustle'.

Even if Musk no longer commands quite the same measure of quasi-Messianic loyalty from his former army of crypto enthusiasts, his biography – possibly more myth than fact by this point – is emblematic of modes of capitalism characterised by personalised charisma and heroic action. One might expect this model of capitalism, centred on the figure of the swashbuckling billionaire, to be very far indeed from Max Weber's influential envisioning of it as a realm of 'specialists without spirit, sensualists without heart' – 'society devoid of charisma'.

Yet Weber also identified forms of capitalism 'much closer to the charismatic sphere of experience'. In *The Protestant Ethic and the Spirit of Capitalism*, he famously articulated a vision of modern and Western capitalism as profoundly shaped by the 'worldly asceticism' of Calvinism in which, as sociologist Anthony Giddens puts it, 'the moral impulsion deriving from the [latter's] commitment to the achievement of salvation' is focused 'upon economic activity'. The result of this transmutation has been a 'sober bourgeois' capitalism based upon and perpetuating continuity, rationality and systematicity and functioning via dispassionate, depersonalised action in a disenchanted world. As such, it's come to be associated particularly with technocracy, or what political scientist Timothy Mitchell has referred to as 'the rule of experts'. Under such stable, impersonal systems, according to Weber, 'capitalism is identical with the pursuit of profit, and forever renewed profit, by means of continuous, rational, capitalistic enterprise.' Moreover, the archetypal inhabitant of this rational, disenchanted cosmos is none other than *Homo economicus*, that preternatural embodiment of rational self-maximisation who's long served as the basis of economics' empirically impoverished understanding of human social relations.

Alongside such sleek and more-than-a-little-unrealistic envisionings of human economic behaviour, Weber also described other modes of capitalist action. For example, he discussed 'the capitalistic adventurer' whose actions are 'predominantly of an irrational and speculative character, or directed to acquisition by force, above all the acquisition of booty, whether directly in war or in the form of continuous fiscal booty by exploitation of subjects'. (He saw modern financial capitalism as having not unimportant affinities with this charismatic model.) It's worth noting here that for Weber, charisma was a primarily political category. Alongside 'rational' and 'traditional' grounds,

Weber saw charisma as the basis of one of three archetypes of 'legitimate authority'. Where the first is the foundation of modern technocratic bureaucracies and the second of hidebound traditional forms of rule, charismatic authority is inimical to enduring structures in the first place.

Weber described charisma as the 'great revolutionary force' of history, fundamentally opposed to established order and antithetical to the forces of routinisation that would seek to tame it. It's less a basis for solid forms than a catalyst for change that, except in rare moments of enduring turmoil (for example, the Chinese Cultural Revolution), tends to quickly burn itself out. In this way, it's fundamentally about heroic action in moments of rupture. Per Mazzarella, it's both world-destroying and world-disclosing. While Weber emphasised its hostility towards, and foreignness to, the economic, I'd argue we're living in an increasingly anti-technocratic and anti-economic moment, where disruption for disruption's sake is in many places the order of the day in both political *and* economic spheres. It's in this light that we need to think through the rise of both charismatic currencies and charismatic (or explicitly anti-economic) economies. Here the rise of meme coins can shed some important light.

ACCORDING TO THE Slovak sociologist Dominik Želinský, capitalism has oscillated between rational and routinising technocratic forms on the one hand and chaotic and disruptive charismatic forms on the other. In this context, the longer term tendency towards charisma, which began with the decline of Keynesianism and the end of the Bretton Woods system of international financial arrangements in the early 1970s, has intensified rapidly in recent years with the rise of populist and authoritarian alternatives to technocracy across the globe. Alongside impersonal forms of economic action dedicated to this pursuit by means of 'continuous, rational, capitalist enterprise', we now often encounter modes of personalised, heroic economic behaviour 'dominated by [a] numinous belief in business [and political] leaders (rather than [in] an impersonal system)'. The latter are, moreover, commonly characterised by a disruptive and often transgressive focus on 'profound individual [and collective] rebirth and change of identity and rapturous emotions mustered through collective rituals'. Indeed, the past decade or so has ushered in a new paradigm based on personalisation, charisma and appeals to explicitly anti-rational heroic and disruptive economic activity.

Such action can occur across multiple scales. It can, of course, take the form of the heroically disruptive interventions practised by prominent businessmen and politicians (and businessman-politicians) such as Musk, Trump or Javier Milei, the firebrand Argentine leader, as embodied perhaps by the totemic chainsaw brandished at economic regulation and societal decorum by the first and last of these. Yet it can also comprise both collective and solitary action by ordinary individuals. Examples of the former include the GameStop short squeeze of January 2021, in which the retail investor users of the subreddit r/wallstreetbets caused major financial losses for a number of large hedge funds and other institutional investors. More recently and less salubriously, such interventions halted play at several WNBA games when sex toys were thrown onto the court by crypto aficionados seeking to promote the eponymous meme coin Green Dildo Coin, which had, according to *Vanity Fair*, been 'launched the day before the first dildo was thrown'.

On an individual level, the paradigmatic form of charismatic anti-rational economic action is hodling (a backronym from 'Holding On for Dear Life'). This term was famously coined by a drunken poster to an online bitcoin forum in December 2013: he was rationalising holding on to his Bitcoins in the face of a collapsing market and his own embarrassment at being 'simply not good enough to beat the professional traders'.

Anthropologist Yathukulan Yogarajah, who's done extensive field research in the badlands of 4chan and other dark corners of the internet, describes the rise of hodling as a key moment in an ongoing 'subversion of economic reason' among crypto investors. According to Yogarajah, hodling 'is one of the most important ideas within the crypto world… The ideal hodler…will not cut their losses and sell when traditional financial wisdom might say otherwise'. Where *Homo economicus* buys low and sells high, Yogarajah highlights a 'popular comedic mantra on 4chan: buy high sell low'.

This 'remixing' of economic reason, Yogarajah argues, foregrounds 'the general feeling that crypto is, to put it crudely, drunk finance'. Indeed, from the perspective of the traditional financial world, it's pure lunacy. But for hodlers, it's a courageous intervention against a world that's otherwise stacked against them. Moreover, it's a means of cultivating the 'extreme uncertainty and volatility' that are the preconditions of profiting from meme coins. Only under such conditions can 'placing a small amount of money…see over a 1,000 per cent increase (or a loss of 100 per cent)'. Where actors motivated solely by received versions of economic rationality would see only madness or frivolity, Yogarajah identifies a powerfully charismatic (in the sense of anti-economic) attempt to reorient an unfavourable playing field in one's favour. In such a frame, meme coins are not frivolous in the slightest; instead, they're matters of financial life and death.

I WANT TO conclude by briefly relating these forms of emergent economic unreason to my own ongoing research into monetary forms in Zimbabwe. This southern African nation, mired in economic crisis since 1997, has witnessed the destruction of its national currency via hyperinflation in 2008–09 and repeated failed (and failing) attempts to reintroduce a national currency over the last half decade. In the last dozen years, Zimbabwe's economy has dollarised and dedollarised and dollarised again, going from a largely cash economy to one where 96 per cent of transactions were done electronically back to one where, in 2025, 70 per cent of transactions are now again being done using cash in US dollars.

Almost invariably, when I broach the possibility that Australia might have something to learn from Zimbabwe, the slightly nervous response has been more or less the same: 'But Australia isn't Zimbabwe!' An associate editor of an online outlet for popular academic publication was even more sceptical: 'The area that most needs work is the lesson from Zimbabwe. I'm not sure I understand the issue, nor whether it has any relevance to Australia.' Freighted in such responses is the notion that there's a difference in kind between economic reason and rationality here at home, and the unreason and irrationality that Australians might imagine exists exclusively out there in the largely informal economies of the developing world. Similarly, my Zimbabwean friends regularly refer to their country's economy as a 'circus', a 'funhouse' or a 'freak show' – and for years have looked wistfully to the West as the locus of economic reason, longing for 'a central bank that isn't campaigning all the time' (notably, this was said before Trump began to actively meddle in the affairs of the American Federal Reserve System) and money that 'doesn't require loyalty' but 'simply works'.

Some anthropologists (most famously Janet Roitman in her 2023 book *Anti-Crisis*) caution against overdrawing the contrasts between what one might term crisis and non-crisis economies, noting that significant convergence exists between the two. One telling example is the parallel between the Zimbabwean Government characterising its new, putatively national currency, the Zimbabwe Gold or ZiG, as the basis for a charismatic narrative of economic nationalism and resilience and the ways in which $TRUMP and other meme coins are attempting to mobilise affective communities of users.

But perhaps a more profound and disturbing aspect of this convergence is the underlying economic nihilism it signifies. The convergence of the ZiG and the meme coin as affective projects highlights the growing sense of exclusion from pre-existing systems of wealth generation among many young people in the *developed* world. It bears emphasising the degree to which anti-rational charismatic and heroic economic action are not simply the fellow travellers of populism, authoritarianism and/or fascism but in fact derive from the growing sense among many young people that the economic systems that worked for their parents and grandparents will no longer work for them – that rational behaviour and, by extension, technocracy more broadly have become dead ends.

Anthropologist Annaliese Milano Merfield notes that 'the crypto community largely comprises young people who view their financial prospects as bleak – especially when held up against the wealth and opportunities enjoyed by their parents at a similar time of life'. She suggests, moreover, that 'their efforts to build financial alternatives to existing forms of money and finance have undermined the state's role in mediating the value of money and the flow of capital'. Ironically, in some ways, this growing constituency appears to be less rational and pragmatic and more given to economic unreason than the Zimbabweans, who have been forced to deal with their circus economy for nearly three decades. Nonetheless, this rising tide of exclusion highlights the degree to which meme coins, far from being some sort of freakish sideshow, are in fact utterly central to understanding economic (and, alas, political) life in the contemporary world.

The lesson here is not a happy one, but it is a necessary one. If we're unable to rebuild confidence in the power of the rational workings of the economy to contribute to general welfare – in the ability, that is, of measured economic action to lead to lasting wealth – we'll face a rising tide of economic and political nihilism that goes beyond questions of mere left and right. In this new world order, measured and rational interventions may well be replaced by radically disruptive, charismatic economic and political action as a kind of revivified propaganda of the deed.

Chris Vasantkumar is a Senior Lecturer in Anthropology in the School of Communication, Society and Culture at Macquarie University. His scholarly work has been published in journals such as *Economy and Society*; *The Journal of Cultural Economy*; *Theory, Culture & Society*; *Environment and Planning D: Society and Space* and *Critique of Anthropology*. He is also the co-convenor of the Future of Money Project, funded by the Social Sciences and Humanities Research Council of Canada. Since 2018, he has investigated the crisis economy in contemporary Zimbabwe, with a focus on the collapse of trust in state currency and its effects on middle-class attitudes towards money, planning and the future. He is currently at work on a manuscript about more-than-human theories of exchange.

IN CONVERSATION

Age of the tech empires

Artificial intelligence and the new colonialism

Karen Hao and Carody Culver

In 2025, the research firm Gartner predicted that worldwide AI spending would reach US$1.2 trillion. By September of that year, America's largest companies – Meta, Microsoft, Amazon and Alphabet – had already spent more on AI than the US Government had on education, jobs and social services combined. The message of these tech giants is one of positivity and progress: AI will change the way we work, the way we communicate, the way we live. But for award-winning journalist Karen Hao, the gap between PR spin and reality is as stratospheric as those spending stats. In her 2025 book, Empire of AI, *she draws on her intrepid reporting from around the world to tell the real story of what's going on at OpenAI – the company responsible for ChatGPT and bankrolled by Microsoft – and in the sector more broadly. In this conversation with* Griffith Review *Editor Carody Culver, which has been lightly edited and condensed for clarity, she reveals the extractive, growth-at-any-cost mindset shaping this transformative technology.*

CARODY CULVER: For many of us, it feels like generative AI came out of nowhere when ChatGPT emerged in late 2022. But as you explain, decades of research and internecine theoretical debates precipitated that moment, and a big part of how we understand AI and its threats and opportunities is down to the term *artificial intelligence*. How did the discipline come to be given this name, and how has this shaped the way scientists and the general public understand what AI is?

KAREN HAO: When it was called 'artificial intelligence', it was the decision of a single person – an assistant professor at Dartmouth University called John McCarthy – and it was against the advice of his mentor, who thought it would be a very, very confusing name, in part because there's no scientific consensus around what human intelligence is… But this did really reframe the way researchers were thinking about what they were doing. That was the reason, in part, McCarthy wanted to use the term: previously he was calling it 'automata studies', but…he wanted people to be more ambitious and really think about how to create human intelligence in computers. It totally changed the way scientists think about it, and it totally changed the way…people who are investing in this technology think about it.

And then, of course, the public naturally conflates AI with this idea that somehow scientists are recreating another species, or at the very least recreating something akin to what they see in science fiction portrayals in Hollywood: these Frankenstein-like human variations that go rogue. And all the debates around 'Is this technology existential, is it going to be smarter than us, is it going to completely do away with our need for brains?' are tied to the conception that this is somehow akin to us and to our intelligence.

CC: One of the things that really struck me in the early chapters of the book is how the development of any technology, AI being a prime example, is often presented by those researching it as inevitable. It becomes entwined with these vague notions of human progress and benefiting humanity. But then you cite the work of two MIT researchers and Nobel Laureates, Daron Acemoglu and Simon Johnson, who argue that no technology is inevitable. Why is that the case, and why are we so fixated on the idea that it *is* inevitable?

KH: They've been doing research for decades around historical technology revolutions and what actually leads technologies to be created in the first place, and there are a couple of conditions that need to happen: there needs to be a rallying ambition around a particular idea, and there needs to be enough capital and political will to make it happen. So, the technologies that end up being created are almost always the conception of the rich and powerful, because they're the ones who have resources to put behind their ideas.

Just from that, you can see that technologies are not inevitable, because there are plenty of other ideas in the world that are just not given the resources or the political backing to manifest… And because it's usually the rich and powerful who end up shaping the conception of technology, [that] technology…often is really self-serving to those rich and powerful people…sometimes intentionally, sometimes unintentionally.

CC: You make it clear that there are all these shifting forces behind the scenes, these powerful elites, and as the field of artificial intelligence developed, two camps emerged: the symbolists and the connectionists. Each of these two camps – I was so fascinated by this – had a different idea of what 'intelligence' means, which led to two different ideas about how to advance AI research. Could you talk about those two different ideas and why the connectionists ended up being the team that won the race?

KH: The symbolists believe we're smart because we have knowledge – so if you want to recreate human intelligence in computers, you should create machines that are encoded with databases of knowledge. The connectionists think we're smart because we can learn…so they thought we should build machines that are analysing data and learning from that data. In the early era of the AI discipline, the symbolists were winning in part because [their ideas] seemed to align better with people's understanding of how intelligence emerges.

But in 2012, there was a key breakthrough in the connectionist realm called 'deep learning'. Three researchers showed that by using software called 'neural networks' – deep neural networks that have multiple layers for analysing data – they could essentially effectively recognise images at a higher accuracy than had ever been previously done. This became very commercially interesting to the tech industry, so Google acquired the company that the researchers formed…and started pumping a lot of capital into the connectionist approach.

As more and more industry money started going into the connectionist approach, they started reaping more and more benefits for their bottom line by imbuing deep learning into not just image recognition but self-driving cars and automated translation. Google ultimately enhanced its ability to target users with ads through search, and then yet more money went into deep learning. Connectionism became unbelievably well-resourced compared with symbolism, which just died on the vine – all grad students going into AI stopped studying symbolism and started studying connectionism and, more narrowly, studying the specific types of neural network architectures that were useful for commercial applications. So, over time, the industry has completely distorted the landscape of ideas within the AI research field to align with a commercial agenda.

CC: That leads us to OpenAI, the company at the centre of your book. Years before Elon Musk donned his red MAGA cap, he was very worried about what he saw as the existential threat posed by AI. When the AI research lab DeepMind was acquired by Google in 2014, Musk was convinced this was going to be the beginning of the end because Google would put profit above everything else. Then he met Sam Altman, who at the time was president of a startup accelerator company and a rising Silicon Valley star. How did that lead to the creation of OpenAI, and what made OpenAI initially seem like it was going to be a different kind of tech company?

KH: Musk was very concerned that Google was developing this monopoly on AI researchers after…the acquisition of DeepMind… Altman was just a very strategic, politician-like character, and as the head of Y Combinator, he was trying to spray his investments in a lot of different domains, [such as] nuclear fusion and different types of biotech – he identified AI as another trend that he wanted to get his hands on. He started to cultivate a relationship with Musk and echoed a lot of his concerns, saying, 'The best way to counter Google is to just build a lab of our own that stands for something fundamentally different.'

And so OpenAI was created as a non-profit. It was meant to be transparent, collaborative, democratic, open source. But the foundations from the very beginning were rotten because it was also a project of ego: both Musk and Altman conceived of the lab in part because they were like, we're the good guys, we want to be the ones to save humanity from evil Google. And that element of corruption then festered and led to a complete one-eighty on their mission.

CC: The Sam Altman playbook seems to be 'I'll just tell people whatever they want to hear and then go off and do my own thing', which, as you demonstrate in the book, led to complete chaos behind the scenes at OpenAI. In those early days, it had all kinds of projects on the go but no clear direction. Then, in 2019, these rapid shifts thrust the company into the public eye.

What happened during that time, and how did it begin to change the way OpenAI was perceived by the industry and the public?

KH: In the AI field, Musk and Altman were viewed with scepticism because they don't actually have AI research backgrounds... On top of that, OpenAI approached AI development with a very particular thesis: take existing techniques in the field and scale. That also gave it a bad reputation because in the research world, taking existing things and throwing spaghetti at the wall to see what happens is not exactly considered innovative. And in those early years, there wasn't really anything to show for this approach.

But then a couple things happened: they created GPT-2, which was two generations before ChatGPT and was the first inkling that there might be something interesting about large language models. And they created a for-profit to sit within the non-profit. Altman officially became CEO of that for-profit, and then they had a $1 billion investment from Microsoft. People start paying a little bit more attention, [realising that] large language models seemed like an interesting idea...and that money could potentially be raised by pursuing this approach because it was catching the interest of big, deep-pocketed companies.

CC: You'd been reporting on the field of AI at *MIT Technology Review* since 2018, and then in 2019, shortly after all this happened, you embedded with OpenAI for three days to write a company profile. What sparked your interest in OpenAI, and what did your experience reveal to you about the inner workings of the company?

KH: I noticed that the research system was starting to orient slightly around open AI's approach of scaling and around large language models specifically. I thought the company was beginning to have influence over what kind of AI was developed as well as potentially what kind of AI would be commercialised. Very, very early on, they were already building bridges with policymakers, so I also thought they would have pretty substantial influence on whether policymakers understood AI development and [whether] the public would understand AI development.

How I pitched [my profile] to OpenAI was, well, you've undergone a lot of changes, so maybe it's time for you to reintroduce yourself to the public? They really liked the idea initially. What I found was...this is a project of altruism, *and* this is a project of ego. I was talking with these researchers and [realising that] they're not interested in this just because it could unlock transformative benefits for people – they're also interested in being the ones to do it, which then started making me ask more questions about what was driving their decisions. Then I realised they were highly secretive, highly competitive, still saying they were a non-profit even though it was clear by now that they had some kind of commercialisation plan on the horizon. Part of the reason why they maintained lip service to the non-profit was because it continued to accrue a lot of goodwill in the public [eye]. That was a fundamental disconnect, and I felt like it should be pointed out. That's what I ended up writing about, and they did not speak to me for three years.

CC: The truth hurts. And Sam Altman feels straight from central casting: he's this kind of Messianic tech leader, he's got seemingly unwavering self-belief, he can charm and persuade all the right people at the right time. One of your two epigraphs in the book is from his blog in 2013, where he wrote that the most successful founders don't set out to create companies but are on a mission to create something closer to a religion. Your analogy in the book for the ways these tech companies operate is *empire*. Could you explain why this analogy best captures what's going on?

KH: First of all, these companies have amassed an extraordinary amount of political and economic power to the point where they're pretty much more powerful than other nations in the world, except for maybe the US Government. You could also argue that they're becoming more powerful than the US Government, because [it] has absolutely no interest in being a counter to them and their ambitions. From that perspective, we need to stop thinking of them as just businesses. They are political actors, geopolitical actors, and their actions have consequences for people all around the world in the way that no government would.

But the *way* they've amassed that power is where I see so many parallels with the way empires amass power. They extract an extraordinary amount of resources, most of which are not their own, and they rewrite the rules to suggest [these resources] were always theirs. They exploit an extraordinary amount of labour, not just in the production of AI... AI itself is being designed right now as a labour-automating technology, so it erodes workers' rights on the way in and on the way out. They monopolise this knowledge production by snapping up all these AI researchers and distorting the scientific field. They are essentially re-forming that field in their image. Whatever science comes out is good for them and continues to perpetuate their ability to keep doing whatever they're doing, and [the] kind of research that would undermine their efforts is censored. Last but not least, they engage in this existential arms-race narrative where they have to be an empire, but a good empire, because there are evil empires in the world, and they, as the good empire, are ultimately on a civilising mission to bring progress and modernity to humanity.

CC: It's interesting too because Sam Altman is one of the tech elites who's talked recently about universal basic income – 'AI took all the jobs away, but it's okay because UBI [universal basic income] can help everyone survive.' I wonder what your take on that is. If these people are so disconnected from the reality of normal life that they come out with these grand announcements when what they're actually doing is destroying the social contract...

KH: UBI to me is just such a weird – it's literally just the welfare state, except that in Silicon Valley's conception of it, they don't pay taxes to the government to enable a more democratic version of UBI where it's actually accountable to the electorate; [instead,] they're the ones that distribute the money. It's just privatising something that should be public. It's like when Elon Musk created The Boring Company to reinvent transportation, and he's talking about *subways*. And you're like, no, we already have that – it's a public good and you're just making it worse.

CC: This notion of zealous belief is such a strong throughline in your book – not just belief in charismatic leaders like Altman but belief in the possibilities of technology. Key to your narrative is this long-running disagreement between two different camps of believers in the tech space: the doomers, who are concerned with AI's existential risks, and the boomers, who believe that facilitating technological progress is a moral imperative. Boomers seem to be winning, but their mission is incredibly expensive, and there's a lot of talk at the moment about whether we're in an AI bubble – NVIDIA just got a market capitalisation of US$4.4 *trillion*. What are your thoughts on this? Is the bubble going to burst?

KH: I think it's about to implode – in part because the premise of the business succeeding is people finding *that* much value in AI that they'd pay *that* much money for these technologies, and then the companies will turn a profit, or those companies monetising people's intimate data at enough of a margin that they become profitable. We're not seeing either of those things happening. Generally speaking, people are not adopting AI at the rate companies need, [nor are they] willing to pay for AI at the rate companies need. And, technically speaking, the technology is pretty limited in terms of which types of tasks it can actually help people with. One of the problems is that it's not accurate... [It's] being pushed into law, into finance, into healthcare, into all these areas where accuracy is really important. But thus far, the adoption is being sustained by people's lack of understanding of the laws of the technology, not by actual evidence that it'll be beneficial.

Once the evidence plays out that it's less worth dealing with the errors of the technology than it is to just constrain where the technology is adopted, the adoption bubble will deflate. It could be really horrible for the global economy – because the money that's invested into this endeavour is coming from people's retirement funds and university endowments... Public market investors I've spoken to have pointed out that they think the bubble will be even worse than the real-estate bubble because with the real-estate bubble, it was one industry that went boom, but with the AI bubble, eight out of the ten richest companies in the world all have their valuation currently over-indexed on AI. We've never had that kind of consolidation in the market on a single thing.

CC: It's terrifying. You talk a lot in the book about OpenAI's obsession with scale, which I guess is one of the things that got us to this point. When they train their large language models, they're so fixated on scaling up that they just keep pumping in more and more data, so the quality of that data has diminished with time. This has led to them setting up content-moderation factories in developing countries, where grossly underpaid workers sift through absolute junk.

KH: This is one of the things I think is not effectively understood. Some people don't even realise there are people in these countries being exploited in the first place, but the other misunderstanding I commonly confront is people who say, well, the internet is kind of like that anyway – social media has reams of people who are poorly paid, but [without them] we wouldn't be able to have social media.

I have lots of problems with that argument, but AI is quite different in that you wouldn't need all these content moderators if you took a different approach to AI development. It specifically becomes a problem when you take the scaling approach and you try to scrape the whole of the English-language internet to train your systems, because then you start scooping up all this awful content, and your datasets are so large that they become incomprehensible… None of these companies have effectively figured out how to filter out the grotesque content from the internet…

The best way to filter it before it reaches the user is to filter it on its way *out* of the model rather than on its way *in*. So, they filter in and out, but they know that the filtering in is imperfect, so the filtering out is like a second catch. We also know that it's imperfect because now people are having AI psychosis due to problems with ineffective filtering on the way out. Then you end up having all these content moderators who need to train that filter by annotating any possible example of the type of content the filter should be blocking, which then requires them to wade for eight hours a day through awful, awful content and end up psychologically traumatised.

CC: There are devastating environmental impacts, too. AI models require physical data centres to run, and these centres use colossal amounts of energy and potable water. Again, this comes down to an obsession with scaling and disproportionately affects countries in the Global South, particularly Chile. You describe Chile as 'ground zero' for a new scale of extractivism. How have these technology data centres changed in the wake of the AI boom, and why have countries in the Global South become the targets for tech companies to move in, extract and then move on?

KH: The data-centre movement is unlike anything we've ever seen before. The modern internet is obviously also built on data centres, but previously, the pace at which data centres were expanding roughly matched the pace at which they were improving their efficiency. So most developed countries were seeing a flatlining in energy demand or a decline in energy demand, even as more data centres were being built. Now, the pace has dramatically exceeded any efficiency gains, so we're seeing a historic uptick in the amount of energy that needs to be consumed globally. Almost all that uptick is due to the data centres being built. These companies have run out of land and energy and fresh water for supporting this, especially in places that have those resources, because, at the same time this is happening, climate change is accelerating.

That's why they're pushing into some of these communities: there's just not enough land in the US now; in a lot of developed countries, communities are pushing back more aggressively, and then it's more easily escalated to the English-language media, which is really bad for the companies. So, if they move to another country where there's less press, or the press is writing in languages that are less international, at least they can manage the PR more easily.

A lot of these developing countries *want* the data centres because they think it [represents] economic opportunity. They don't realise when they enter the bargain that they're also giving up an extraordinary amount of their natural resources. If they realise it, they somehow think it's still worth it – many of them live with a legacy of colonialism [and have] this mentality of 'in order to be relevant to Global North powers, we just need to open our resources up for extraction'. So, you end up with this dynamic that repeats the dynamics of the past, where certain countries are just being hollowed out for their resources to continue perpetuating this expansion that ultimately is completely unsustainable for the planet and for people – not just in the environmental and public health senses but also in a pure physics sense. The laws of physics tell us that there is literally not enough stuff to be consumed in the world to support the trajectory these Silicon Valley companies say they're on.

CC: You talk a lot about people in the AI industry who have tried to speak out about these issues and have been silenced. But you also tell some really galvanising stories about people who are fighting back in different ways, like activist groups in Chile or an Indigenous couple in New Zealand who created their own LLM to help new generations of speakers learn *te reo* to try to revitalise the Indigenous language. Do you think we'll start to see more of this pushback?

KH: That's actually been one of the things that's been most heartening about being on tour: I've met so many people who are engaging in this kind of resistance. It's not just anti-AI; it's anti–Silicon Valley's model of tech imperialism in general. I think a lot of people, whether they fully grasp the difference between AI versus their smartphone or social media or whatever, generally feel that they have a crappy relationship with technology these days.

One of my personal missions with the book is to help people connect the dots for what they need to push back against – and how. There's so much opportunity for the average person to add their voice to shaping how technology is developed in the first place, and often people don't realise that they have access to that kind of influence. You have the ability to go to your city council and tell them, 'This data centre project, it's not being transparent about the amount of energy and fresh water it's using from our community, so we cannot allow it to proceed.' That gives them something to grab on to, to operationalise the feeling they already have. People really get the issues, and they have the energy to do something about it. It's just a matter of directing that energy.

Karen Hao is the author of *Empire of AI* (Penguin, 2025) and an award-winning journalist covering the intersections of AI and society. She writes for publications including *The Atlantic* and leads the Pulitzer Center's AI Spotlight Series, a program training thousands of journalists around the world on how to cover AI.

NON-FICTION

Uncanny virtue

The moral bankruptcy of effective altruism

Richard King

I FIRST HEARD Peter Singer speak at the University of Western Australia (UWA) in the summer of 2009. The subject was the ethics of what we eat, and the tone of the talk was open and generous. Some in the audience were hardcore animal-rights people, as one would expect at a Singer gig. But the philosopher's message was that ethical eating is, in fact, a pretty complex matter, bearing not only on animal welfare but also on economic justice and the environmental impact of agriculture, and that what counted as ethical behaviour in one sphere was often difficult to reconcile with ethical behaviour in others. His advice was therefore to do what we could, advice I for one resolved to follow before hogging into the free wine and nibbles around the Beaux-Arts-style reflecting pool.

The second time I heard Singer speak was in the winter of 2015, and the atmosphere was chillier all-round. Again, the venue was UWA, and (again) the philosopher's demeanour was congenial. But the message had a harder edge. The lecture was entitled 'The most good you can do' – based on Singer's new book of that name, a follow-up to *The Life You Can Save* (2009). Beginning with a sketch of our scandalous levels of global inequality, Singer argued that morally serious people should dedicate a percentage of their income to charities and NGOs in the business of alleviating the poor world's suffering.

He then drove home this ethical imperative with one of those thought experiments of which utilitarian philosophers are so fond. Would we, Singer wanted to know, pass by if we saw a young child drowning, for fear of ruining a new set of clothes? And, if not, then why do we pass by children who are starving or sick in other parts of the world, when our money could give them the food or drugs or infrastructure they need to survive? Being a morally serious type myself, but philosophically a bit wet behind the ears, the question struck me like the runaway tram in another famous ethical scenario. Even now, when I think of it, I imagine a small child facedown in that reflecting pool, while Perth's intelligentsia sip pinot gris and savour their complimentary vol-au-vents.

Though the phrase was not on my radar at that time, Singer's talk distilled the central tenets of the movement known as effective altruism (EA). And while I continued, whenever I could, to tithe my meagre writer's income to favoured charities and NGOs, as per the movement's principles, I admit I didn't think much more about it over the ensuing seven years or so, save to reflect occasionally on its rather simplistic approach to economic justice. Until, that is, another tram came careering down the ethical tracks, in the form of a woolly-haired entrepreneur with a house in the Bahamas worth US$35 million and some very, *very* dodgy accounts.

Sam Bankman-Fried was the CEO of the cryptocurrency trading platform FTX. He was also in a whole heap of trouble. FTX had entered bankruptcy proceedings in November 2022, leading to rumours about fraudulent transfers of clients' funds within the company. That furore led, in turn, to panicked sales of the company's 'native' token, FTT, which was followed by a wave of customer withdrawals that FTX had no hope of covering. The world's largest cryptocurrency exchange signed a letter of intent to acquire the company and then speedily withdrew the offer after taking a look at its books, which by that stage were also in high demand from the relevant US Government agencies. In December 2022, Bankman-Fried was arrested in his Bahamas home and extradited to the US to face criminal charges of, inter alia, wire fraud, commodities fraud, securities fraud and money laundering. In the subsequent trial, he was found guilty on all counts, ordered to pay $11 billion in forfeiture and sentenced to twenty-five years in the slammer.

None of which struck me as especially odd – at any rate, not initially. Corruption, after all, is hardly an aberration in the world of finance capitalism, a system that seeks high private returns, as opposed to high social or moral ones, and so is always subject to skulduggery. Perhaps, like Aesop's scorpion, Bankman-Fried was merely being true to his nature. But here's the thing. The disgraced CEO was not just a devotee of EA but apparently so committed to the cause that he was willing to mislead FTX's investors and imperil the savings and livelihoods of its clients in order to fulfil its objectives. Indeed, and as many commentators have noted, including fellow EA acolytes such as internet billionaire Dustin Moskovitz, there seemed to be a deep connection between Bankman-Fried's catastrophic dealings and the social and philosophical movement to which he'd become attached as an MIT undergraduate. This was not a tale of simple greed.

Or not of simple greed alone. By the looks of that mansion in the Bahamas, Bankman-Fried was doing okay for himself, and we must always allow for the possibility of a bit of 'charity washing' in this space, as well as a bit of 'ego defence' in the light of behaviours one knows to be wrong. But trying to squeeze the FTX scandal into the old anti-capitalist narratives is in my view too naive an approach. EA and its undergirding philosophy are far more interesting, and far more troubling, than the greed-is-good libertarianism of the merely rich and powerful, curled up in their New York and London apartments with *Atlas Shrugged* or *The Road to Serfdom*. Yes, we should keep one hand on our wallets (ethically speaking) when addressing this issue. But EA tells us something about our times that critiques of neoliberalism alone do not, while also giving us a better sense of where we might be headed next.

At the very least, the EA phenomenon affords a fascinating glimpse into the minds of those who are coming to the centre of social and economic life in the second quarter of the twenty-first century. For those of us who are anxious about that direction of travel, getting it into frame is therefore essential.

THOUGH SINGER'S PARABLE of the drowning child sets out the core morality of EA, the movement is as defined by its *approach* to this imperative as it is by the imperative itself. For William MacAskill and Toby Ord, the two Oxford University academics who have done the most to shape the EA movement, it is not only morally virtuous to allocate a proportion of one's income to the cause of greater global equality, as Bankman-Fried did with his Future Fund and as Ord encourages others to do through his and MacAskill's charity, Giving What We Can; it is also necessary, or at any rate desirable, to grow that income as big as one can. For hardline effective altruists, to seek the highest return on investment with a view to increasing the size of one's donation (in absolute rather than percentage terms) is objectively more altruistic than earning (and thus donating) less – a neat reversal of the Christian parable in which an old woman is deemed more generous than her rich neighbours for giving her last pennies to the temple treasury.

It is for this reason that EA has tended to encourage its followers to pursue a life in big business, and that, in keeping with its consequentialist underpinnings, it stresses reason and evidence in pursuit of maximum moral impact. One of the first EA non-profits was the charity-assessment company GiveWell, which focuses on the cost-effectiveness of the charities it evaluates, as opposed to more conventional metrics such as the percentage of an organisation's budget earmarked for overhead expenses. Similarly, MacAskill's 80,000 Hours, which is named for the average amount of time a typical human being spends in paid work, provides advice on which careers are likely to result in the largest positive social impact. As MacAskill himself puts it in *Doing Good Better* (2015): 'We very often fail to think as carefully about helping others as we could, mistakenly believing that applying data and rationality to a charitable endeavour robs the act of virtue. And that means we pass up opportunities to make a tremendous difference.'

Some critics of EA make the straightforward argument that its acolytes are engaged in reputational laundering, and that its simplistic approach to complex issues of socioeconomic justice is as likely to worsen the condition of those it seeks to help as it is to improve it. But even if we take it at its own best estimation, we may still experience some ethical queasiness at the attempt to link the creation of extreme wealth to the alleviation of poverty. There's a trace of the old 'trickle-down economics' in this prospectus, which in people of my age and background may trigger memories of Margaret Thatcher running out John Wesley's line about earning, saving and giving 'all you can'. (Alas, on the Methodists' support for the working class, the Iron Lady proved something of a heretic.)

Certainly, the ethos of the EA movement is a thoroughly individualistic one. The structural reasons for poverty and inequality are rarely on the lips of its advocates, who can seem almost childlike in their approach to such matters. Through its liberal use of the second-person pronoun ('the most good *you* can do', 'the life *you* can save'), it evinces a puritanical streak – 'progressive neoliberalism' in a dark, stark ensemble.

More deeply, EA's philosophical origins are inseparable from industrial capitalism. Beginning from Jeremy Bentham's proposition that the moral action is the one that produces the greatest happiness for the greatest number, utilitarianism is so called because the things that *produce* happiness are said to possess 'utility'; and utility, for Bentham, could be measured in money. This early vulgarity does not sit well with some contemporary utilitarians, many of whom are politically progressive, but it survives and thrives in the calculative ethos that defines the consequentialist tradition of which utilitarianism is a part. Utilitarianism is a moral system shot through with the abstracting logic of capitalism.

From this perspective, EA can be seen to perpetuate the very system that causes the problems it seeks to redress, in a way that is analogous, perhaps, to the 1990s craze for microfinance, where many poor households in the Global South were pushed into the debt economy as the price of their economic salvation. Even in successful cases – cases in which EA can be shown to have resulted in the alleviation of material hardship – the underlying logic of capital comes to colour humanitarian endeavour, fundamentally changing our ideas of what it means to act charitably. Karl Marx's concept of the commodity relation, where social relationships are mediated through exchange, robbing them of their 'sacred' character (a concept caught in the charge that a person 'knows the price of everything and the value of nothing'), is relevant in this connection.

As we've seen, MacAskill seeks to ground charity in 'data and rationality', but a mindset as wedded to rationality as EA in its hardcore form is apt to undermine the very solidarity – the ethos of care and loving-kindness – without which charity ceases to be meaningful, and without which Singer's drowning-child scenario would cease to have any impact at all. When people recoil from the effective altruists' attempts to *quantify* suffering or to calculate *returns* on altruistic *investment*, it is this they are reacting to. EA evinces a *mathematical* morality – one in which the levels of abstraction needed to meet the movement's stated objectives threaten to undermine the 'virtue' at the centre of the enterprise.

In short, there's something slightly *inhuman* about this species of humanitarianism, or something slightly *uncanny* about it. And it is, I'm convinced, this uncanny quality that speaks to the current historical moment.

DERIVED FROM THE Latin words *abs* and *trahere* ('away from' and 'to draw', respectively), *abstraction* describes the retreat from materiality – from the palpable, physical stuff of the world – and is a fundamental feature of the human condition, one without which we could neither store complex information in our minds nor convey it to others through the system we call language. But as central as abstraction is to our humanity, it is apt, in its 'higher' forms at least, to 'draw us away' from the human scale, with consequences that are unconducive to our flourishing.

Channelling the nineteenth-century economist and utilitarian philosopher Henry Sidgwick, Singer invites morally serious people to take up the 'point of view of the universe' – that is, to contemplate as objectively as possible 'the most good you can do' for others. But this 'universal' calculus is liable to lead in some troubling directions. What if I modified Singer's drowning-child parable to include a wealthy philanthropist? In the event that he's drowning, too, and assuming I can save only one person, whom am I morally obliged to save? The universe (as constructed by Singer, in a way that appears to beg the question) says I should save the philanthropist, on account of his capacity to save so many others. Most decent people, it seems to me, would run towards the child without thinking – and tell 'the universe' to fuck off.

If this extension of Singer's parable seems a little tendentious on my part – too literal-minded an approach, perhaps, to an innocuous thought experiment aimed only at pinpointing a moral inconsistency – consider how, in recent years, the EA movement has embraced 'longtermism': an ethical system that emphasises humanity's future trajectory, and as good an indication as one will find of where this highly abstract tradition in moral philosophy is likely to lead. Widening Singer's moral imperative from the current global population to those who will be born in the future, this trend is by no means unanimously popular among effective altruists, but the publication of Ord's *The Precipice* (2020) and MacAskill's *What We Owe the Future* (2022) suggests that it's growing in stature. Moreover, and according to a recent report in *The Economist*, long-term EA projects now account for something in the region of 40 per cent of EA investment globally, with money flowing towards space colonisation and the development of new and safe AI – projects some distance from supplying poor countries with schools or antimalarial drugs, though no less worthy of moral attention in the utilitarian 'universe'.

Much of this future-directed energy is focused on existential risk, and on the risks of AI in particular. Ord especially has made this issue a central plank of his moral system, arguing in *The Precipice* that humanity is now uniquely exposed not only to natural catastrophes such as asteroids and super-volcanoes but also to 'anthropogenic' ones such as nuclear war and engineered pandemics, and that it is, therefore, our moral duty to safeguard humanity against those risks.

No doubt that view will find favour with many. But seen in the context of the EA movement, with its focus on altruism and charitable giving, it is a bizarrely abstract line to take. To put non-existent human beings on the same moral plane as the existing ones will strike many reasonable people as obscene – a recipe not for altruism in any recognisable sense but for total moral immunity and lack of accountability. Surely it is no coincidence that prominent 'transhumanists' such as Nick Bostrom have set their shoulders to the EA wheel. When you spend your days dreaming of 'extreme longevity' or physical and cognitive 'augmentation' or of escaping your physical body altogether and becoming one with the universe, why wouldn't you spruik for a moral system that casts you in the role of humanity's hero?

Indeed, and carrying on from that, it seems clear that EA's turn towards longtermism is both the cause and the consequence of a society in thrall to powerful new technologies. The broligarchs of Silicon Valley are among EA's most vociferous backers, while Elon Musk has said that its tenets are close to his personal moral values. It's tempting to put this trend down to personalities, to the 'uncanny' demeanour of the broligarchs, with their apparent lack of social skills and emotional intelligence. But it's also clear that the EA movement taps into a more general mindset – one linked, no doubt, to our habituation to digital technologies and the disembodied sociality to which they've given (or are giving) rise. A moral system, after all, does not exist in isolation from the society from which it emerges, and our society is now changing in ways that are unhelpful, antithetical even, to social solidarity and individual flourishing. EA is a 'morbid symptom' of that disorder.

Perhaps another thought experiment will be useful. Faced with the classic trolley problem, in which a subject is asked to decide whether or not to divert a tram from a track with five people on it to a track with only one person on it, most people say they would pull the lever. But when the subject is asked to say if it is acceptable to *push* a man in front of the tram to save those other five lives, most people answer in the negative. Entire books have been written about that discrepancy (as it might appear to a utilitarian), but really there's no great mystery. Once you've adjusted the thought experiment to eliminate *intention to kill* as a factor, by arranging for our human obstacle to be tied to a sidetrack that *rejoins* the main one, it becomes clear that the key difference between the two scenarios has to do with the prospect of *physical contact*. In short, it's easier to imagine ourselves killing someone if the killing is technologically mediated. Technology changes our 'moral intuitions'.

My point is not that utilitarians are cold killers, or cold killers *in potentia*; nor is it that people are in danger of becoming utilitarians without realising it (though there are studies suggesting that the appetite for 'utilitarian sacrifice' is rising sharply among the young). My point is that there's a deep connection between the 'disembodied' morality of EA and our technological situation. For all that it looks, at times, like a cult, the EA movement is a reflection of our age.

AS SOMEONE WHO does most of his moralising on the left, I find myself half in sympathy with those who dismiss the EA movement as (at best) the fantasy of socially maladjusted nerds or (at worst, and much more likely) a species of reputational laundering. But as Simon Cooper has written in *Arena*, such responses don't go far enough, in that they fail to take account of broader transformations – *material* transformations – in social life. Indeed, it may be that progressives themselves are influenced, in part, by the calculative ethos that has given rise to the EA movement, and that in arguing back against that movement they are channelling the same quantificational reasoning. The observation that only around eighty-five people are now in possession of as much of the world's wealth as the poorest half of the global population is not without its polemical uses. But what's *really* being compared here – when so much of that 'wealth' is speculative, tied up in intellectual property, abstract rights and production royalties?

Similarly, the charge that a billion people now live on less than a dollar a day assumes that having twice that amount would go some way towards rectifying that injustice, which perhaps it would, in a narrow sense. But like capitalism itself, quantification of this kind rides roughshod over social realities that are not reducible to income levels. Such criticisms of capitalism are reflections *of* it and apt therefore to miss the main point, which is that the capitalist system is founded on an abstraction that takes no account of our deepest needs or the rich multiplicity of human cultures.

How did the left (or what's left of it) come to think in these utilitarian terms? As I suggested earlier, the answer is social: the twin realities of neoliberalism and technological mediation have engendered a 'dashboard' view of the world. As heavy industry was offshored in the West in the 1980s and '90s, and educational meritocracy came to the centre of social life, economic production became increasingly abstract, based upon data, texts and images, and reliant on new communication technologies such as the PC and the internet. Some thirty years on, this more abstract reality is now a generalised phenomenon, not least because of the intersection of social media and mobile telephony. If our politics is increasingly abstract, it's partly because we live in a world no longer defined (or less defined than it was) by face-to-face relationships. As Cooper writes:

> The moral injunction to concentrate on those who need help the most and to bypass the needs of those immediately in front of us is easier to follow when the flows of capital, people and information that characterise the form of life today allow us to ignore those more grounded settings of place, body and community. Glued to your phone, you probably wouldn't notice the drowning child anyway.

None of the arguments I've made in this essay are intended to suggest that Singer's parable of the drowning child and the new set of clothes doesn't have some moral force. It *did* have force and continues to do so. But the force it has, whether we like it or not, is tied to our ability to imagine a scenario in which we're called upon to act – to act *directly* – to save the life of another. My guess is that, for many people, the parable will prove more forceful still if both the setting and the child are familiar to us. In my own case, that setting is UWA, where I first encountered Singer's scenario, and the child I'm saving looks remarkably like my own daughter, who was six at the time and learning to swim.

Is the life of a child in a Sudanese village worth any less than the life of my daughter? Objectively, no; subjectively, yes. And committed as I am to redistribution, I cannot accept a moral system that invites us to obliterate that distinction. This is not because it hurts my feelings to be told that my children are no better than yours, but because my feelings are not to one side of what it means to be a human being with the capacity to act ethically. To suggest that they *are* to one side of that capacity is to arrange not only for a dispensation in which a tech billionaire can claim to be acting morally by ripping off his customers, but also, and far more importantly, for a world in which we are becoming uncanny both to one another and to ourselves. It is to arrange for a bankruptcy far deeper than the one that originated beneath that woolly hair.

Richard King is an author and critic based in Fremantle, WA. He is the author of *On Offence: The Politics of Indignation* (Scribe Publishing, 2013), *Here Be Monsters: Is Technology Reducing Our Humanity?* (Monash University Publishing, 2023) and *Brave New Wild: Can Technology Really Save the Planet?* (Monash University Publishing, 2025). He can be found at his website, bloodycrossroads.com.

FICTION

The landlord's son

Rhianna Boyle

THE LANDLORD'S SON arrived unannounced, just before dinner. Mia saw him from the window as he crossed the paddock from his own house. Passing the tank, he rapped his bony knuckles down the rungs. *Keep an eye on the tenants*, his father had told him. Despite his youth, the boy took his responsibilities seriously. He began a leisurely inspection of the garden bed. Mia had dug it the day after she moved in. Three tomato plants had survived the hot weather, and the fruit was almost ripe. The landlord's son reached to squeeze a tomato, with a touch both tender and proprietorial. He pulled it off the vine and popped it into his mouth.

He knocked on the front door. Mia waited a moment and took a breath. She'd begun to dread the sound of his knock and the uncanny regularity of his mealtime arrivals.

'Oh, hi, Simeon.'

'Hi, I'm sorry to disturb you again, but I need to speak to you about something.'

He used one foot to dislodge a mosquito from his calf, then scratched the site with his toenails. Like most of his family, Simeon was habitually barefoot. Finding themselves heirs to a large property, no longer viable for cattle but secluded from the prying eyes of authorities, the landlord and his brothers had filled the paddocks with a sprawl of sheds and caravans. Tenants were referred by word of mouth, a last lifeline before everything fell apart.

The landlord went to great lengths, collecting people from the railway station or prison gates, or moving their belongings with his own trailer. He was a kind man, people said. He would do anything for you. The family no longer walked barefoot out of poverty, like their hard-grafting ancestors. Shoes were a social imposition on those whose time was not their own. Among the lantana and rusting car bodies, the landlord's family were their own masters now.

'Do you need to come in?' Mia was conscious of an instinct to recoil, as well as the need to keep it from her voice.

Without being invited, Simeon sat down at the dining table. Mia had cleaned underneath it one day and found the names of the landlord and his brothers carved in childish letters.

'I just came to remind you that your rent is due. I mean, it's due on Monday, but I'm reminding you as a courtesy because I'd like to avoid the same situation we had last month, if we can.'

Mia's car had broken down, and she'd put off paying him. That was when his evening calls had begun.

'It should be fine this time, it's just with the car and –'

'Yes, I realise you've had some difficulties. I'm just doing it as a courtesy to you.'

Simeon's voice had a studiously maintained gentleness. His wandering fingers found a tomato seed caught in his whiskers. He rubbed it away.

'How's your dad?' Mia asked.

'Well, he could be better, obviously. They moved him into hospice care last week, so I've had to take on more of his responsibilities.'

He sighed, showing the weight of his heavy administrative burden. While he never admitted to loneliness, Mia suspected it was this, as well as an inability to cook, that brought him to her house on flimsy pretexts.

'Oh no, I'm sorry to hear that.'

Though it was never discussed, they both knew that soon the boy would not be merely the landlord's son. He would inherit all of his father's property.

'Hi, Simeon!'

'Tommy, my mate!'

Her son, abandoned by his father, lived in awe of this older male. She left them alone while she finished cooking dinner. Tom came into the kitchen, under instruction, to ask for three glasses and some very hot water.

Mia found them conducting a science experiment in which Tom had to hold his fingers in water of different temperatures. The finger in the hottest water was red and swollen. Simeon's games were often tests of strength and endurance. With Mia, Tom was by turns hostile, distracted or in tears over small discomforts, but he submitted stoically to the older boy's demands. Without instruction, he'd managed to absorb the rules of masculine behaviour.

When the baby started crying, Simeon went to lift her out of the cot. Tom pulled his fingers from the water. His gaze flickered briefly across Mia's own. Simeon was better with the baby, gentle and indulgent, but his voice when he lifted her up was the same one he used to remind Mia that the rent was due. Mia steeled herself.

'We're just about to eat, if you'd like some?'

'Thank you, that'd be lovely.'

During dinner, Simeon explained the theory behind their science experiment. Each finger had been preconditioned, so transferring them to the same lukewarm glass produced different temperature perceptions in exactly the same environment. The philosophical implication was that there was no such thing as reality: sensory perception was all relative.

The family business gave Simeon time to read widely, and he could speak at length on any topic. He seemed genuinely baffled that other people lacked his store of arcane facts. Audaciously, he'd even advised Mia on childrearing.

She interrupted Simeon's monologue to tell Tom to put his pyjamas on.

'You're sleeping in Nanna's room,' Simeon told the boy.

'It's *my* room.'

'That's my nanna's old bedroom. She *died* in that room.'

Simeon thanked Mia for the meal, then left to pick his way back through the paddock.

Tom woke up later that night, haunted by Nanna's restless ghost.

Mia was restless, too, angry because she couldn't speak her mind. *You let people walk all over you*, her mother had once told her. They were outside on a grey day. Her mother was attached to an oxygen tank, grey-faced in a white hospital gown, having cajoled Mia to wheel her out for a cigarette. These had been some of her parting words.

MIA HAD THOUGHT living out of town would be peaceful, but she often felt besieged. A man inexplicably called Ferret – she didn't know his real name – lived in the nearest shed. The night before, she'd seen him outside, stoking a large bonfire and drinking a stubby. She glimpsed firelight on his hard-bitten face. He turned up his speakers by increments, until she could feel the music vibrate through her floor. Ferret was expecting party guests, she thought, but after more than an hour, no guests had arrived. She tried to put the kids to bed, but Tom kept calling out for her, and then the baby woke up.

Mia's stepfather would invite his friends home late at night so they could keep drinking after the pub kicked them out. Mia would appear in her nightie, tearful, the party pooper trying to spoil their fun. For the first time, she'd encountered the contempt of grown men and its accompanying underbelly of danger. She'd been braver as a child, begging for the music to be turned down. Now she knew how it would go.

She heard a knock and opened the door to find Ferret.

'How's your evening?'

'It's okay.'

'I'm just having a few beers, if you want to join me?'

Mia realised that she was the guest Ferret had been expecting. The fire and the music were meant to lure her.

'Um, I have the kids.'

'You can bring them.'

'Actually, they're in bed. The music is pretty loud.'

Her fellow tenants were mostly single men. She knew they gossiped about her, the stuck-up new chick with her big house, given to her by the landlord because of the kids. She watched Ferret's face fall.

'Yeah, no worries. I can turn it off.' He held up his hands, placating.

The silence was a relief, but she feared she would pay later. Any small victory seemed to go on a giant cosmic tab, to be recouped in sudden, unpleasant ways.

HER CAR BROKE down on the way home from shopping. She pulled over into the weeds on the side of the road and tore open a packet of crackers to keep the kids quiet. She hadn't yet told Tom they'd be walking home. Stupidly, to avert a battle in the moment, she'd let him go to the shops without shoes.

She opened the boot and surveyed the shopping. Factoring in the baby, she knew it was more than she and Tom could carry between the two of them. Some of it would have to be abandoned to spoil in the heat.

She left her daughter's door open.

'I'll be back soon.'

She didn't want Tom to see her cry. Her own mother's crying had usually come after the drinking. There were stretches – sometimes years at a time – when she was a good parent. Then, usually when a new boyfriend appeared, she seemed to lose interest, as if having a daughter were a hobby she'd outgrown. Mia dreaded repeating the pattern but at times found herself besieged with vivid fantasies of doing something worse, like leaving the kids on the side of the road and starting a new life somewhere else.

A car pulled up next to hers. It would serve her right if they were abducted just as she was wishing them away. She ran but saw that it was Simeon. He leant in the window to talk to Tom.

'It's okay,' she called. 'I'm just here.'

In the seat of Simeon's ute, buried under the shopping and with the air conditioning on, Tom was thrilled to be allowed into his hero's inner sanctum. Mia wondered if Simeon could see that she'd been crying.

Once he'd helped her carry the bags inside, she had no choice but to invite him to stay. He stretched out on the carpet to play with the kids.

Mia knew there was a rift of some sort between the boy's father and his uncles. Simeon had mentioned a girlfriend. Sometimes he implied that their bond was a serious one, on a higher plane of maturity than those of their peers, but then he would forget his own narrative and parody the girl in an arch falsetto. Mia was familiar with her in passing but rarely saw her at the house. She didn't know why, when Simeon's father was dying, Simeon's girlfriend would be absent.

Then there was Simeon's mother, the woman who really did leave her child for good, by way of a car and a tree on a straight stretch of road.

They made a sad trio of dinner-party guests, Simeon looking for a mother, Tom for a father, and none of them getting what they wanted. Perhaps she'd been too hard on Simeon, Mia thought.

After dinner, she watched him put on a puppet show for the baby, with witty asides aimed at her and Tom. He finished his performance, then stood abruptly and stretched. His eyes caught something on the architrave above the kitchen door. He put his thumb against the wood and it gave way like paper.

'Termites. We sprayed before you moved in, but they're all the way through the place.'

He went down the doorframe, then along a floorboard, crumbling the wood with his hand and leaving a trail of pulp.

'Bastards.' He wiped his hands on his shorts. 'Thanks for dinner.'

He left without looking down at the mess he'd made.

IN THE MORNING, Mia was surprised to see her car being towed into the yard. Ferret emerged from the vehicle in front, followed by Simeon from her own. Ferret would repair the car free of charge, Simeon told her. He'd arranged it all. He left them to it – just Mia and the man she'd rejected, perhaps angered, a few nights before.

She was wary of Ferret's hunger for company and the way his hopes for a less lonely future might fall, with single-minded focus, onto her. In the past, mistaking someone else's need for her own inescapable destiny, she'd thought this was love.

Ferret, clumsy in courtship, possessed a calm that eluded him outside the bonnet of a car.

'So, I hear Sim is pulling your house down.'

Perhaps this was a kind of revenge for him, to casually deliver the devastating news. Her shock must have been obvious.

'He did find some termites last night,' she said.

When he looked up from the bonnet, Mia glimpsed the shadow of a smirk.

'Apparently, the place is full of them. He's going to gut it and start again with the frame.'

Mia had wondered if Simeon's evening calls were a source of gossip among the male tenants – imagined sleazy assignations by a kid with an unfair advantage, a boy acting as silverback. She'd got her comeuppance now.

'Yeah,' Ferret said. 'I heard that's always been the plan. They thought about it after the grandmother died, but his old man wanted to put you in there instead. The kid's less of a soft touch.' He looked back under the bonnet and twisted something languidly with his pliers. 'I'm surprised he never told you all this. I've got plenty of room at my place.' He gestured towards the shed. 'Or I was thinking of just hitting the road again. Make a fresh start. I could do with some company.'

WHEN SOMEONE KNOCKED late that night, Mia's first thought was that it was Ferret, there to collect his dues. But it was Simeon.

She'd been awake anyway, going over everything she'd missed. He'd eaten her food, knowing what was to come. She'd put his bad manners down to a youthful lack of insight, but maybe he'd simply taken all he could while he had the chance. The image of him lifting the baby, with his saccharine patter, made Mia's skin crawl. His occasional kindnesses now looked like pre-emptive penance.

The boy on her doorstep appeared to have the swagger knocked out of him, though. He sniffled and wiped his nose with his hand. Mia smelt alcohol, though she'd often heard him disparage people who did not value their own mental clarity.

'Dad's dead.'

He seemed to be wielding the words for the first time, testing their power.

'Oh no, when?'

'I've just come back from the hospice.'

He began to sob loudly, and there was nothing Mia could do but put her arms around him. He accepted her sympathy greedily, squeezing her tight.

'Both of your parents are dead, aren't they?' he asked.

'Yes.'

'How do you even *go on*?'

'I don't know. You find a way.'

'I don't know what to do.'

'You don't have to *do* anything. You just keep living.'

Mia's parents had died without the good grace to leave her a large inheritance. Her response just now had been curt, but the boy didn't seem to notice. He paused, pondering what she'd said.

Just keep living, he repeated, as if the phrase contained some deep wisdom.

She couldn't send him back out into the night in this state. She pictured his mother, the car and the tree.

'Why don't you sleep on our couch?'

She got him a blanket.

'Thank you. I appreciate it.'

Asleep, he looked like a child, despite his moustache.

As the sky lightened, a thought appeared: she'd let Simeon walk all over her, just like her mother had said. Her kindness stemmed from a weakness of character, but nonetheless she'd saved him from himself. She'd fed him when he was lonely, then hugged him as he'd cried. That kind of bond was hard to ignore. She'd inadvertently incurred him a debt that could not be repaid with eviction. In the morning, Simeon was gone. The blanket was left trailing on the floor.

LATER THAT WEEK, Mia saw a line of cars arriving for the wake and the family in black, picking their way across the paddock in uncomfortable shiny shoes. She saw Simeon with his girlfriend, who seemed to be back in the picture now.

Tom had developed a newfound fascination with death. He leaned on the windowsill, watching.

'Will we have to move now?' he asked. 'Because he's dead?'

'I hope not. I don't think so. I think Simeon will let us stay.'

'Because he's our friend. Isn't he, Mum?'

'Maybe.'

THEY FINISHED EATING the tomato crop, and Mia planted out the bed with broccoli. The weather was unusually cool and clear. Even if they had just one more year in the place, it'd be long enough for them to catch their breaths.

After a few weeks, she noticed that Simeon didn't visit anymore. She put the rent in an envelope and pushed it under his door. The house was peaceful without the prospect of his evening calls. Grief could make people do strange things, she thought. His girlfriend's car was often parked in the driveway now, and she saw the two of them out pulling weeds in the landlord's garden. Things had returned to their natural order.

A letter arrived. Mia wondered if he'd paid someone to draft it; the language sounded so precise and bureaucratic. She was hereby informed that she was being given notice to vacate the property no later than a period of two weeks from the date of the letter.

It was signed *Sincerely, Simeon Collins (Landlord).*

Rhianna Boyle's fiction and science writing have appeared in *Griffith Review*, *The Lifted Brow* and *The Big Issue*.

NON-FICTION

Splitting the bill

The moral cost of the ultimate profession

Patrick Mullins

A COUPLE OF years ago, after too many years too casually spent as a casual academic, I went to work at a law firm. It was in need of a writer, and, for a steady wage, I was willing to pretend to be one. For a time, the change felt daunting, and I eased that feeling by making a mental note of its differences with my old workplace. At the firm, everyone was smartly dressed and spit-polished; at my university, there were professors who padded the corridors with rumpled hair and bare feet. At the firm, everything was urgent; at university, nothing ever was. The firm's tearoom was stocked with gleaming coffee machines, bowls of fresh fruit and individually packaged Tim Tams; the only things stocked in the faculty tearoom at my uni were cockroach baits and dead cockroaches.

Money was the most visible difference. At the uni there was none – certainly not for casual tutors – but at the firm it was everywhere. The man who recruited me had prefaced our discussion about salary by saying the firm had money to burn, and once I'd started, I saw fires wherever I turned. On my first day, the woman showing me around said that the firm could take care of my dry-cleaning, if I needed; that it would reimburse my gym fees, if I wanted; that I should order Uber Eats on the firm's tab, if I was working late; that I should charge an Uber to the firm, to get me home after dark. On my first Friday, I was startled to hear balloons bursting nearby. A stampede of passing solicitors soon corrected me. 'It's Bolli time,' said one, grinning. 'Bollinger,' clarified another, en route to the popping corks.

The largesse was astonishing. But it was also clear that the money was being burnt with purpose: the 'perks' were snares to keep people in the office for as long as possible, working as much as possible. There was no excuse, no godly reason, after all, to waste time going to the café downstairs when a coffee machine was just across the hall. Knowing you could get a free Uber home made it easier to work late: no need to be concerned about waiting in the dark for a bus that might not come. Even that champagne, I suspect, was probably opened to head off anyone planning to leave early for a Friday drink.

The tech companies who first laid these snares were never particularly circumspect about how it all worked for them. 'Our philosophy on perks,' wrote Mark Zuckerberg in 2009, in a booklet Facebook provides to all new employees, 'is that we want to provide services that are utilitarian and help people with things they need in order to help them focus on our long-term goals.' He continued:

> Everyone needs to eat. Everyone needs to do laundry. Everyone needs health services. Everyone needs to get to work. If we can make these parts of our lives easier, then it helps us to focus on what we're trying to accomplish at work and it makes us all more productive.

The firm I worked at was never as forthright – it didn't need to be. Every solicitor in the place was smart enough to know that the business was predicated on how long they could stay sitting at a desk. Younger solicitors had to quickly accustom themselves to working sixty to seventy hours in a week. Older hands regarded it as a test of who really belonged. Zuckerberg had articulated the prevailing ethos: 'Greatness and comfort rarely co-exist.' When someone at the firm left – to join another firm, to join the public service, to do something else – the attitude among some of those who remained was, *sotto voce*, that they'd chosen to be comfortable instead of great.

Lisa Pryor, at least, would be cheering those departing solicitors on. Formerly a journalist, now a psychiatrist, Pryor wrote an acerbic and insightful book about the phenomenon in 2008. In *The Pinstriped Prison*, she described how big firms in finance, law and consulting hoover up talented young people, seducing them with perks, paycheques and prestige, simultaneously training them to accept that their waking lives should be devoted to work. The tragedy of it, she argued, was that too many of these people would never be able to leave those firms. By the time the novelty of the perks had worn off, they would have become habituated to the grind, come to rely on the money and status. They were imprisoned.

Pryor wasn't suggesting we grieve for those lawyers and accountants and consultants, with their six-figure salaries. She was suggesting, rather, that we reflect on the broader social cost of losing those bright and talented people to businesses defined by narrow commercial interests. 'Rhodes scholars who trained to be geographers, engineers, ministers, and scientists are forsaking these professions for management consulting,' she wrote. 'Maths PhDs are snapped up by investment banks, leaving Australian mathematics in a state of crisis.' What if, instead, those bright youngsters used their education and talents to work on policy development or scientific research, solving the dilemmas that would make their societies better?

The question Pryor posed seemed, to me, to be most acute for lawyers. Not just because of the unique privileges – in terms of expertise, salaries, status – that come from membership in what one historian has termed 'the ultimate profession'. Not just because, at a fundamental level, the obligation of the legal profession is to serve the administration of justice, which affects everyone. Most of all, that question seemed acute because all the solicitors I met at my firm, and those I knew and came to know in other firms, had wrestled with it. Their answers suggested there was no easy division, or indeed one-off choice, between private-sector money and societal contribution. Rather, it was an ongoing part of their daily lives, an accommodation of means and ends, a playoff with that most finite resource: time.

LAURA HAS LONG been one of the smartest and most driven people I know. She's always combined a ferocious work ethic with a very serious sense of purpose: when she commits to something, she gives it everything. From her earliest days of studying to become a solicitor, she was dedicated to making a meaningful contribution to the world. As a student, she worked for a local women's refuge; she filled the four-month gap between her final semester and graduation by moving to Ghana and doing pro bono legal work for a human rights NGO. After graduating, she joined the public service in Australia to work on women's rights and Indigenous affairs. After a few years, thinking she could contribute more elsewhere, she moved to the UK. Brexit had upended everything, especially the future of immigration and asylum law, and Laura went to work for an NGO to help settle it. The pay was low and the hours were long, but the work was worthwhile, she tells me. For two tumultuous years, she was in the thick of it – and enjoying it, too.

But a turning point came when she sat down to do her taxes one night. 'I realised that I hadn't earnt enough that year to qualify for repaying my HECS debt,' she says. 'That hit me. I thought: *Oh, I need to go and make money.*'

It wasn't that she suddenly felt deprived or money-hungry, Laura explains. She was perfectly happy – well, happy enough – to go on renting a room in the three-bedroom flat that she and her husband shared with two other couples. She thought her work was valuable. She didn't feel short-changed by the job's meagre salary, nor aggrieved by its demands.

Rather, she realised that, unless she earnt the funds to make repayments on her HECS debt, the debt would grow. In light of this reality, working for an NGO took on new significance. Laura was happy to make a sacrifice in the moment, accepting a lower salary so she could do consequential work that gave back in some way. But was she just as happy to have that sacrifice reverberate in years to come, costing her in the years ahead, setting up a future where she would be wrestling down that ballooned HECS debt at the same time as she was trying to have and raise children? And what about when she and her husband decided to buy a house? The thought of trying in London was sobering; the thought of trying in Australia was not much better.

Working for an NGO, Laura decided, was unsustainable. She had to move. But her persistent desire to do meaningful work limited how far she was initially prepared to leap. For this reason, Laura became a government lawyer, spending the next two years doing high-volume litigation. She believed it was valuable. But a final break – what she jokingly calls her 'move to the dark side' – came when her family circumstances changed. She returned to Australia and joined a major commercial law firm. After another two years, she moved to a different firm of similar status. Now in her early thirties with two children, she has no intention of returning to NGOs or the government.

'It just doesn't pay enough,' she says. 'I come from a comfortable but not well-off family. I remember thinking that I didn't have the backing to go off and do endless study, or work at NGOs, and not earn money.' Coupled with these circumstances, now, is a dissatisfaction – perhaps aided by hind-sight – with the work she did in those NGOs and in government. 'It wasn't outcome-driven. You didn't get a result for what you did. You'd petition the government to do something, and they wouldn't do it. You'd write a paper, and no one would read it. I found that really frustrating.'

For a time after her move to the dark side, Laura thought it still might be possible to make her contribution. Each of the firms she joined had formal pro bono programs that provided legal services on a free or a much-reduced-fee basis. Recipients ranged from individuals unable to afford legal services to organisations that raise matters of public interest to charities and not-for-profits whose overriding purpose is the public good. Pro bono work ostensibly allows solicitors like Laura to contribute to that good while drawing a decent salary. For the firms that offer formal pro bono programs, pro bono is also a way of keeping lawyers at their desks, working. Laura's firms explicitly encouraged her and her colleagues to do pro bono work. They even incentivised it – one made completing a hundred hours of pro bono work the precondition for being eligible to receive a yearly bonus.

'Law firms push it,' Laura says. 'They want you to do it. But they want to make money more.' What this meant, in practice, was that a solicitor of Laura's experience and seniority could do only diminishing amounts of pro bono work. 'The moment you settle into your practice group and become valuable to that team, with a full workload, it becomes impossible [to do it],' Laura says.

Workload was the problem. Most big firms require their solicitors to generate seven-and-a-half billable hours per day. To generate and deliver those hours, though, a solicitor will need to work an additional three hours, *minimum*. This means a ten-hour day is almost *de rigueur* – and that's if everything runs smoothly. If a colleague needs additional support, if a meeting runs long, if a client questions a bill and time has to be written off, then the day can get even longer. Every minute spent talking to a colleague about kids or weekend plans, every minute spent eating or going to the bathroom, must be added on top.

For Laura, that workload is exhausting but also exhilarating. She tells me she thrives on the intellectual stimulation of responding every day to new problems, on the pressure brought to bear by the consequences, the money and the culture of the private sector. She doesn't see her work as narrow. She doesn't feel trapped. But its structure and demands have forced another reckoning, she admits, on how and where she can contribute. 'I don't do any pro bono work now,' she says. 'I've come full circle from my "saving the world" kind of self. I just can't, anymore. It's impossible. If I did it, I wouldn't be seeing my children on the weekend.'

Her contribution, Laura says, is now made through her children. 'I made the decision that, while my husband and me didn't have enough money for me to go and get a master's and then go and work for an NGO in Burundi, I *could* go and get enough money so that my children could have that choice. And that's why I think I'll stay at a commercial firm, now: because I want to give my children the option.'

IF LAURA HAS redirected where and how she contributes to the public good, then Fiona has kept it front of mind. Her career seems anchored by a strong sense of moral purpose. Fiona spent years giving pro bono legal advice at a youth centre. She did academic research and writing with one of Australia's leading legal scholars and worked overseas at a local NGO, advocating for migrant workers who have suffered abuse.

Fiona's eventual departure from NGO work was not prompted by money. The empathetic dimension of work was wearing her down, personally, and her role was changing to be more focused on fundraising. It required skills she thought lay outside her strengths. When she was headhunted by a major commercial law firm, saying 'yes' seemed a straightforward proposition: the timing was right.

Experience in that firm was illuminating. 'It's such a simple business,' she says of private law. 'The money is so central.' But after a year and a half, she wasn't comfortable having money remain so central in her life. 'I wanted to do something that I cared about, something that would make a difference,' Fiona says. So, she decided to leave: 'I wasn't sure, if I stayed, that at sixty I'd be proud of myself.'

For the next three years, Fiona worked in the public service, advising on legal outcomes for new policy. It was work that was purposeful, contributing to something bigger than herself. But there were orthodoxies, too, that sat at odds with Fiona's views of a legal professional. An expectation of regular transfers and promotions seemed misplaced: it would mean Fiona had to manifest, almost overnight, a working expertise in a completely different area of law. Nor could she deny that the meaningfulness of her work was much diminished if the government of the day changed policy direction or discounted aspects of legal risk.

After a few years, then, she returned to the private sector, to another commercial firm. The partner who recruited Fiona, listening to her concerns, suggested that a binary between commercial and impactful work might be misplaced. Solicitors in private firms could do work for government, and that work had a public impact – for the good. Solicitors with different mindsets could nudge the culture of private firms, too. 'She talked about skills that can make a difference,' Fiona says, 'and she talked about how you can measure your impact, and being clear about it.'

Fiona is critical of and optimistic about pro bono work. She's direct about how law firms portray it in their marketing materials. 'They talk about it as though it's something great that they're doing for the community, altruistically. But clients will often require that firms do a certain amount of pro bono. They'll put it in the contracts.' She also points out that doing pro bono is part of the professional ethos of being a lawyer – the Australian Pro Bono Centre suggests thirty-five hours per year: 'It's an expectation.' To the obvious question of whether pro bono programs are cynical, Fiona rolls her eyes: 'Pro bono programs allow big firms to feel okay about making so much money.'

But there's a real contribution there, she argues. She describes one pro bono matter currently on her desk: a draft constitution for a new charity. The work she does on that constitution should save the charity time and resources later; doing it pro bono means the charity isn't expending valuable resources as it gets established. 'With pro bono, you know that there is someone who needs help,' she explains. 'And it reminds you that you have these skills, these specialist skills, that not everyone has, and that you can use them to help other people.'

Fiona regards her working at a private firm now as the right place for this stage in her life. She does work that's challenging and interesting and worthwhile for her clients. By setting boundaries around her work hours, she can attend to another of the contributions she sees herself making to the world: taking care of her family. 'I am not saving the world,' she says. 'But I'm working in a place that supports me, at a firm that cares about its people and the community. I have to be content with that. I tell myself that I can still do more – it's just that it's not today.'

ZACH IS AT a different stage in his career from Laura and Fiona. In his early sixties, he made a good living for many years by working at a major law firm.

With his children raised and mortgage long gone, he's now stepped back from the demands of daily legal practice. His preoccupying concern is contributing to the community. Years of working under the tyranny of the billable hour have shaped the way he makes that contribution. He's scathing of how, in the 1980s, he and his colleagues would go to the Salvation Army warehouse to pack Christmas hampers and tell themselves they were 'giving back'.

'What a waste of time,' he mutters. 'It would have been far more helpful to them if we had used our professional skills – the things that we can do, that they can't do for themselves. Not packing hampers. Anyone can do that. We were probably more hindrance than help, too.'

Now, he sits on various boards, does pro bono work for a handful of charities and stresses his determination to be productive on them. He has no interest in a given position because of any status attached to it. Some of the organisations he's involved with reflect his personal interests – libraries and hospitals, in particular – but others have come about because he's been asked and has felt obligated. Zach regards it as important to say 'yes':

> Earlier lawyers – and I'm speaking here about those at big firms, up until the 1980s or so – would be involved in the community all the time. They would be part of the local law society, would be involved in the universities, would be doing law reform work. They would have a charity that they looked after, individually. It wasn't formal. It was discretionary.

He cites by way of example a colleague – much aged, when Zach worked with him – who'd served in the Second World War and would look after the legal needs of his fellow veterans. He would help draft their wills, deal with the old Repatriation Department on their behalf and more – all for free or at sharp discount. 'But that kind of approach fell away as money became more important. The law used to be a reliable, safe, middle-class profession. It still is that – but it also became a lucrative profession, too. That brought with it pressure on people to bill and to focus on budgets.'

For Zach, there's a sense in which his work now is making up for the imbalance that manifested in that environment. It's also personally meaningful to him:

> I was cooked when I finished [as a partner]. Years of fourteen-, sixteen-hour days, weekends – the lot of it. The looking after people and living with big judgement calls, constantly on edge of making a mistake or upsetting a client: it had just done me in. But doing this brought me back. It has been genuinely good for me.

Zach has no truck with the idea that formal pro bono programs are PR exercises alone: 'There's a lot of good work done in them – influential work, too. And if it's good for the firms, who cares? That doesn't mean it's not good for the recipients. Or the people doing it.' Nor is he willing to accept there's a hard distinction to be drawn between pro bono and other legal work. Commercial work can align with the public good, he argues. Expertise generated in the commercial world can be used to help the community. Legal efforts in the early 2000s to provide immediate tax deductions on regular charitable donations, he explains, are responsible for increasing average individual donations in Australia. Work done in the NGOs can also improve what's done in the private sector. The billable hour, he points out, was invented by a Legal Aid solicitor in the US, in the 1920s, to ensure that resources were used efficiently.

'I won't deny there are problems, and I won't deny that sometimes we're too well paid and don't do enough to repay the community. But,' Zach says heavily, 'in my whole career I've not once met a solicitor who didn't have it on their mind that they should be making some contribution to the community – that they should be doing more. That, surely, is a good thing.'

ZACH'S POINT RESONATES. When I speak to Lisa Pryor about the problems she identified some seventeen years ago, she recalls that, while *The Pinstriped Prison* passed without notice in the accounting and consulting professions, it resonated in law. 'Lawyers felt conflicted. They talked about it.'

Pryor initially describes her book as an 'artefact from a previous time'. But soon she ventures that the rising costs of university study and the ever-growing costs of housing will have made money a stronger influence on the careers people choose. If that's something to be deplored, the solution cannot merely be personal. Pryor insists on the agency of those who feel imprisoned by their careers and our agency, as a society, to alter the factors that create this prison. 'We have more choices than anyone in history,' she says. 'We're better educated, have more opportunities, can do things that earlier generations cannot. We need our bright and talented young people to think about how they will contribute to the world. We need to encourage them to live lives that benefit everyone.'

That means more support for careers that are heavily weighted to the public good and a cultural shift that sees the public good prized above mere commercial returns. It's hard, frankly, to see such a shift in support happening anytime soon. But if I've taken anything from the years I spent working at that law firm and speaking with so many lawyers, it's an awareness of the fierce belief so many had that their profession was also a vocation. They didn't just pay lip service to the administration of justice. Many were intent on seeing justice enacted, on their community and society changing for the better. Money, so many of them said to me, was an outcome of their work – but it was never the most important one.

Patrick Mullins is a Canberra-based writer. He is the author of five books, including *Tiberius with a Telephone* (Scribe, 2018) and *The Trials of Portnoy* (Scribe, 2020), and a winner of the NSW Premier's Literary Award for Non-Fiction and the National Biography Award. His next book, *The Stained Man*, will be published by Scribe in May 2026.

Isi Unikowski

Shopping at Babel

All civilized states have considered it their primary duty to provide for equal weights, measures, and coins.

– REPORT FROM THE SELECT COMMITTEE ON WEIGHTS AND MEASURES (1862)

We're announced by a little bell as we enter.
Behind the counter that guards the door –
above ice creams and a chicken-wire cage that holds the local papers –
a woman in a parka jabs at the register with fingerless mittens
while she instructs her helpers on how to stack wines
they're too young to buy. We order

a firkin of butter
a boll of oats
hobbets of barley.

Bring us, we demand, a sack of potatoes that weighs 14 pounds
to those who live hard by the hills to the west
but 16 for those who live north of the lake
and 18 for those at the edge of the forests; and let them bring us

a todd of wool
an ell of cloth
hogsheads of wine
puncheons of brandy.

For our barbecues, we say, fetch
a chaldron of coal from your yard to the backshop
where light's complicated arithmetic
adds up its columns of dust and shadow.

And if we've sent kids back to school
for an extra year (being forced to learn
how to take the world's measure
in hundredweights and ha'pennies);

if our manifests are covered
in a threadbare dustjacket of avoirdupois
confounding merchants whose tenders collide
over the weight of *a windle of wheat*;

if farmers can't spit and slap hands
over *thraves* and *stimparts*
that mean different things in different counties;

if we refuse decimals for such music as plays on
in *lispound* and *kilderkin,*
leaving nothing in change
to jingle the little pockets of their names, except for

> *a pottle for the woman at the till*
> *a beatment for the boy stacking shelves*
> *a kemple for the child eating an ice-cream on the bench outside;*

let our exchange eddy all the more carefully around
such words, plunged like sticks
into the backwaters of commerce;
a currency that only we tender
to celebrate confusion's adornments.

Isi Unikowski has been widely published in Australia and overseas, including in *Best of Australian Poems 2022* (Australian Poetry). His collections *Kintsugi* (2022) and *Re:Vision* (2025) are published by Puncher & Wattmann.

NON-FICTION

The ridiculous school

On eating the rich and biting your tongue

Fiona Wright

THERE IS A single-sex private school not far from my suburb, where I have lived, now, for close to eighteen years. Across them all, I have walked past its sandstone gates and tennis courts that stretch along the main road, along a smaller back street that bears its name and where its cricket pitch, indoor swimming pool and cadet academy do the same. I have plucked roses – a flower I will never take from an actual person's front yard – from its street-facing gardens, and I have resisted picking up any of the turds my dog has laid there, though I am always, otherwise, a good citizen in this respect. I have taken great pleasure at the sight of its students stuffed into woollen blazers on 40-degree days. I have referred to them (in their absence only) as shits and snots and wankers.

This is who and how I am – and have always been. I want you to know and understand this. It is important to me.

For close to eighteen years, I have walked past this school without ever setting foot on its grounds. I have always spoken of it, on the rare occasions this was necessary, as The Ridiculous School.

The punchline may well be an obvious one. My girlfriend's older son has just started high school, and he is enrolled there.

He loves it, and he is thriving.

HERE ARE SOME things I now know: that the school's grounds, beyond those imposing gates, are large enough that they could comfortably contain at least three of my high school's own in their entirety – and they include six separate cricket pitches. That there are staff employed to patrol the streets of the neighbouring suburbs in the mid-afternoon, purely to ensure those blazers are not taken off in public. That there are swimming trunks (and that is the word they use for them) as part of the school uniform – in the school's colours and with its logo on one leg.

That the admission fee, each year, is equal to what I earn. (I am not, for the record, in any way involved in its payment.)

And also that none of this matters, not in the context of my family's lives. I am, of course and for want of a better word, the stepmother to my girlfriend's children, which is to say that my role is always supportive and not agential. I'm not the protagonist and do not want to be. The problem is that neither can I be antagonistic, nor should I.

I never thought that I would be here. Never imagined I might find myself driving through those massive gates on the occasional stormy afternoon and idling in a queue of European cars as the older boy swings his cricket kit onto my backseat (though I still curse those of their drivers who insist on trying to turn right when they return to the main road). Receiving the school's monthly magazine with its thick, soft pages in my letterbox. Stitching name tags onto uniform trunks, the existence of which I couldn't even fathom until last year. It is unsettling, to say the very least.

And I hate it.

IT IS A strange and uncomfortable thing to have so clear, and to be so conscious of, a class difference between me and my girlfriend's children. These children who are not mine, but something very close to mine, whom I love and tend as family, and to whom I am unquestioned and undifferentiated as kin. To see so often the baseline being set for their expectations of the world and what they consider normal, natural, self-evident – and know that it is so different from mine. So too that they cannot yet understand this. I try not to be defensive about it. I can't help but be defensive about it.

The sociologists Eve Vincent and Rose Butler argue that it is in this 'friction', in the moments of discomfort and discordance within what they term 'cross-class relationships', that the material reality of class – our own, and that of those around us – often becomes most apparent. This is because class is, in part, relational, comparative: I can't help but compare the factors and forces at play across my girlfriend's children's formative years against those that worked across my own (nor can my girlfriend, for that matter – but that's another story). But more than this, the disquiet I feel is at its keenest in those moments when I sense my own life and its conditions being compared – by strangers, or brief acquaintances, by private-school parents – as if they are inseparable from those markers that belong to my girlfriend's boys: The Ridiculous School, the extracurricular activities, the series of au pairs their other mother employed when they were younger. This isn't me and this isn't mine, and I know I shouldn't care what strangers see and assume, but I do.

When the self you see reflected back to you, even briefly, even just in passing, is not the self you know yourself to be: it is uncanny. And deeply unsettling.

I want to eat the rich, not be mistaken for them.

VINCENT AND BUTLER are interested in cross-class relationships because these entanglements have an intimacy – that attempt to truly know someone and all that's shaped them, that sharing of the ongoing, everyday experiences that constitute so much of a life, so much so that they are, in many ways, a negotiation of a way of life – that is tied up in, and illuminates, so many of the emotional aspects of class. They argue not only that class is – like everything we're hesitant to speak about, everything we hold taboo – emotive, but also that emotions are a part of our class structures, something that 'produce and are produced by' class positions and conditions.

What they mean is this: as we are growing up, we learn which sets of emotions are 'deemed appropriate' in particular contexts and settings – a process in which class 'plays a key role', given that different classes have different mores around emotional expression, find different contexts comfortable, or challenging, or ludicrous. And in these formative years, more importantly, we also acquire a set of emotional reactions to class and its inequalities, inevitably shaped by the class conditions in which we are enfolded.

By this reckoning, I know at least a part of my defensiveness and my disdain is all but instinctive, that it is deep-rooted and old. I am the child, after all, of two public school teachers, both of whom were, and still are, vehement believers in public education and equal access to it as a basic human right. Like them, I am a person who does not think it is just, or even socially useful, to separate off the portion of children whose parents can pay from those who cannot, let alone provide whatever facilities and resources and connections that private schools may grant only to some; who finds it abhorrent that public funds – which we have no choice but to pay – undergird so many of them so extravagantly. This is who and how I am – but by Butler and Vincent's reckoning, I did not shape myself this way alone.

It is, of course, difficult to pinpoint the emotional reactions to class that were present in my childhood. Its classed aspects were, as they so often are, invisible to me at the time I was immersed in them most, and so much of our formative emotional life is implicit, rather than directly said, in any case. A few phrases, possibly recurring, possibly just sticky in my child's mind, are all that I can think of: it's alright for some, and they have more dollars than sense. There's a gruffness to both of these phrases, something dismissive. It may not be disdain, but it comes close.

I do remember my first real confrontation with my class position, in the year I started university, when I found myself within a cohort of students – I was studying media and communications, out of a vague sense that journalism might be something that a person who was good at English could viably pursue – who were as incomprehensible to me as I was to them. They had a polish to them, even at eighteen, a more confident way of moving through the world. They wore polo shirts, the men flipping them at the collars, and huge sunglasses perched on the tops of their heads. They carried their books in shopping bags from designer brands and asked if there were cows in Menai, the suburb where I still lived. They were, it turned out, overwhelmingly privately educated: in one tutorial, I made a (yes, disdainful) joke about private schools, and the silence that followed was astounding. I didn't fit in there, and I struggled with the estrangement: I thought the problem lay with me, my eagerness, my brashness, my naiveté. It took me years to figure out that the difference was one of class, that we had come from different worlds and had not yet learnt to see the different landscapes we carried with us and within us.

Perhaps this is where I learnt my defensiveness and my disdain: I had been wounded, and so I grew protective. Disdain is, after all, a much easier emotion to admit to and allow than anger, especially for young women.

BUT HERE IS the problem with disdain: each time I have found myself drawn into conversation with a parent at The Ridiculous School – a parent who has chosen to send their child there, or at the very least consented to the decision – I have felt (and pushed aside) my own resistance, and it has been met with kindness, with interest, with genuine engagement. Of course it has, but each time, especially early on, I have been surprised to find human beings where I expected monsters. I am ashamed of my standoffishness: expecting judgement, I have been judgemental, and that is not who I want to be.

So too this: I spoke recently to a friend of mine, herself a writer, about my confusing and confronting first year of university, and she did a double take. She had studied similar subjects (for similar reasons, I suspect) at a different university, and she had been deeply hurt by the way her cohort had reacted when she revealed she had been privately schooled. I spent all of my school years, she said, desperate to get out of there and find my people, and when I finally thought I had, they dismissed me. For the world that she had come from, which was not of her choosing: she suffered too.

I sometimes think this is the tragedy of childhood: that there is nothing in it any of us get to choose, yet we must hold it within us, forever.

Another recurring phrase from my childhood, which only occurs to me now: my father saying that the one reason to send your child to a private school is that you want them to be surrounded only by people like them.

I still think there is a truth in this, but the more time I (have to) spend with people who have made this decision, the more I think it's not that simple. Few of the reasons I have, in one way or another, been privy to are circumstances that have made me think I might, within them, at least be tempted to do the same. Most of them defer to the kind of upbringing these parents themselves had. They too, that is, are classed emotions, and we will always stand on different sides of their divide.

I AM TRYING to be kinder. I have no interest in being any less vehement, any less angry, any less welded to my ideals – but simply to remember that they are ideals, and that we are all embedded in a system that makes their practice complicated. Or, at the very least, there is often a chasm between ideals and the particularities of any individual, or any family, life. I am trying to do this, even though there is (will always be) a part of me that doesn't think I should have to do this, because fuck it and fuck them. Nevertheless, I am trying.

I want to find a way to want to eat the rich and have civil conversations with them as well – because my girlfriend's lovely boys are not the targets of my disdain, and they must not, however accidentally, be caught in its crossfire. I mustn't ever make them feel monstrous.

WHAT I HAVE instead is this: one of the games my girlfriend's children play on their Nintendo is *Animal Crossing*, which begins with the player's character arriving on an island, overseen by a lazy-eyed racoon, part quartermaster and part business manager, named Tom Nook. Tom Nook offers you a parcel of land, and then a tent, then a simple house, then extensions to it, all of which you have to pay for – or, more precisely, pay off, as he operates entirely by loan schemes – by gathering, harvesting and selling various materials from across the island. When they first started playing, the younger boy, six or seven at the time, was outraged by Tom Nook's mortgages. Incensed that he had to pay Tom Nook increasing amounts of the money he had earnt. And when he protested these financial obligations, I said, without thinking, 'It's because Tom Nook is a capitalist pig!' – a line he later repeated to his other mother, who was distinctly unamused.

It can't hurt them, I guess, to learn in these simpler, more indirect ways – these ways that do not involve their peers, their friends' parents, their actual IRL existence – my emotional reactions to class alongside those of their biological family. It may even, eventually, make these things less invisible, which I still believe is vitally important.

Fiona Wright's most recent essay collection is *The World Was Whole* (Giramondo, 2018). Her first book of essays, *Small Acts of Disappearance* (Giramondo, 2015), won the 2016 Nita B Kibble Literary Award and the Queensland Literary Award for Non-Fiction, and her poetry collections are *Knuckled* (Giramondo, 2011) and *Domestic Interior* (Giramondo, 2017). She was the 2024 Judy Harris Writer-in-Residence at the Charles Perkins Centre, and her debut novel, *Kill Your Boomers*, is forthcoming with Ultimo Press.